Dance until the Music Stops

Books by Esther C. Gropper

Not Far From the Tree: Fictionalized Memoirs
Close Friends: Birthday Poems, Watercolors, Menus & Recipes

Dance until the Music Stops

An Inspiring Guide to Extended Life

Esther C. Gropper

iUniverse, Inc.
Bloomington

Dance until the Music Stops
An Inspiring Guide to Extended Life

Copyright © 2011 by Esther C. Gropper

All rights reserved. No part of this book may be used or reproduced by any means, graphic, electronic, or mechanical, including photocopying, recording, taping or by any information storage retrieval system without the written permission of the publisher except in the case of brief quotations embodied in critical articles and reviews.

iUniverse books may be ordered through booksellers or by contacting:

iUniverse
1663 Liberty Drive
Bloomington, IN 47403
www.iuniverse.com
1-800-Authors (1-800-288-4677)

Because of the dynamic nature of the Internet, any web addresses or links contained in this book may have changed since publication and may no longer be valid. The views expressed in this work are solely those of the author and do not necessarily reflect the views of the publisher, and the publisher hereby disclaims any responsibility for them.

Any people depicted in stock imagery provided by Thinkstock are models, and such images are being used for illustrative purposes only.

Certain stock imagery © Thinkstock.

ISBN: 978-1-4620-5406-0 (sc)
ISBN: 978-1-4620-5407-7 (ebook)
ISBN: 978-1-4620-5408-4 (dj)

Printed in the United States of America

iUniverse rev. date: 12/19/2011

I dedicate this book to my sons, Malcolm and Robert,
my daughter, Laurel and to their generation
who are about to take the lead into the future.

N.B. Quoted sources provided are sometimes lightly edited.

Contents

Introduction	ix
1. You Are Top Priority	1
2. Questions We Need to Ask	9
3. Life as an Investment Folio	15
4. We Are Living a New Kind of Tribal Life	19
5. Taking Personal Inventory	23
6. Meeting and Greeting	29
7. Finding New Interests	35
8. Art of Conversation	39
9. Things You Can Learn from a Donkey	47
10. Health	53
11. There Is a Process for Choice and Change	59
Living for Change	59
12. What a Time We Live In: Changing Mores	65
13. To Exist Is to Change	73
14. Accepting the Changes	81
15. Sunshine and Rain in the Ebbing Years	89
16. Memoirs	93
17. Are Your Juices Still Flowing?	101
18. Stored In Memory	107
19. Imp of the Perverse	111
20. Awaken the Brain	117
21. You're Primed for Adventure	123
22. Sexuality in the Elderly	129
23. Romance and Sex	137
24. Fun-Loving Seniors	141
25. Dealing with Problems	145
26. Re-channeling Emotions	153
On wounded feelings:	153
Anger	154

Loneliness	156
Stormy Weather	158
Recommended for disappointments and for healing a rift in your relationship:	160
27. Choice Is Everything	165
28. Know Thyself	169
29. Learn to Fit In	173
30. Life Is a Ballet Dance	177
31. Stay on the Happy Side	181
Passion and Perseverance	189
One Inspired Person Affects a County	192
32. About the Author	215
33. Acknowledgments	217
34. References	221

Life isn't about waiting for the storms to pass;
It's about learning to dance in the rain.
—Anonymous

Introduction

I decided to write this book after I found myself confronting aging without any indication of what those years would offer or afford me. My parents never reached eighty years, and what I observed of their lives—reading and sharing the daily newspapers, listening to radio programs, and delighting when we brought the little ones to brighten their lives, with the biggest treat being an outdoor drive with a lunch stop at a café—seemed pleasant, but passive. My grandmother, who lived to ninety-six, had still taken pleasure in her flower patch, but the remaining hours were spent in pretty much the same domestic fashion life as my parents. Was that the promise of long life?

Not for me! My body still resonated with high energy, a vibrant curiosity about the world around me, and senses that still served my desire for music, art, drama and books. Nor was I alone. A whole new abundant senior population is searching for activities suitable and fulfilling for their lives.

I was fortunate to have been associated with the Palm Beach State College Institute for Lifelong Learning, in Florida, as a lecturer and presiding officer. I had on-site experience addressing outreach classes at neighborhood residences and on campus. These were not people ready to fit into old patterns of retirement. Theirs was a *refirement*. Their search was replicated across the country.

I want to share my experiences with people seeking an enriched agenda for these years ahead. I want to share the environment we can provide for those years. I want you to know that advanced age offers laughter and pleasure; social and intellectual life along with new and old friends who are ready to share the favors that our added years afford.

Dance Until the Music Stops is intended to guide your passage to an extended lifespan: to make it less frightening or threatening; to make the transition easier to understand; to introduce advantages of independent-resource living; and to share what lies ahead for couples and for singles—namely, that senior age offers splendid opportunities for a good life, a pleasurable life; that community-independent living avoids loneliness and isolation and offers companionship and sophisticated activities that are meaningful while providing services and fulfilling fundamental needs.

Is there pain? Are there sorrows? They, too, are part of aging, as they have always been throughout life. We will confront and work through these while reassuring you of the better days you will have as you plan and participate in the process of living.

Dance Until the Music Stops is replete with humor, real-life stories, anecdotes, and research. Humor is listed first because in our search to find the right way to live successfully, we find that two wrongs don't make a right, but three left turns do ... and what's left of life is dancing until the music stops.

Try to maintain the will so strong in you as you matured;
let it be your mainstay as you assess questions
that will enrich later years.
—Buddhist philosophy

You Are Top Priority

Jacques Brel, playwright and lyricist of *Jacques Brel is Alive and Well and Living in Paris*, identified the two important dates in life: your birth and your death. That said, it's up to you to fill in the drama and comedy that represent "your hour upon the stage and then is heard no more," except in the memory of those who knew you.

How can we fill that time?

Old answers are no longer viable.

We are the first senior adult population with what can be considered an extended generational life span. We are a new generation of an older population with no previous models before us. We have longer lives, stronger lives, and active minds and bodies seeking a new approach to the added years. Quite possibly, this is an evolutionary step up in human development. Yes, we have had elders living into the 90's and 100's before but never as notably as in the contemporary period.

Life expectancy worldwide increased by thirty years in the twentieth century. In the United States, it might be slightly higher. Available census figures show an increase of 4.5 million people in the United States since 1998. The population 65 and over in the year 2000 will increase from 35 million to 40 million (a 15 percent increase) and then to 55 million in 2010 (a 36 percent increase for that decade).[1] One of the messages to be deduced is that society must find ways and means to make longevity a benefit or blessing, not a burden.

The generation now in their seventies, eighties, and nineties is novel.

---

1 Administration on Aging. US Department of Health and Human Services.

Esther C. Gropper

Extended age opens new passages never traversed before; new questions and solutions never considered before; new modes of living never lived before. Because the aging community is reshaping its perceptions and values, old solutions no longer reconcile with older people. Old answers are no longer viable nor are they desirable. For instance, taking refuge with children is old hat; old hat is old stuff. The very word *old* is outmoded. Our senior population possesses vigor and vitality; its members approach life energetically, like lively molecules seeking new arrangements.

Maintaining that high level of energy and interest is a top priority, and it doesn't take a proverbial rocket scientist to figure out why when we live in a youth-oriented culture. Stylists make very little distinction between ages: clothes are cut to fit a good figure—good meaning slim. Meanwhile, on another wavelength, you are urged, cajoled, and pressured to exercise while being lectured on its value every day. If you're in your twenties or thirties, you're eager to keep that size four or six, so you're diligent about the before- or after-work gym program. After that, it's a challenge to stay trim. You conscientiously watch your diet, walk the ten blocks to the bus or train, walk a flight or two of stairs instead of taking an elevator for short stops, keep your body moving more, and adhere to good health routines.

Staying youthful is a state of mind; living a life that keeps the bounce in your step will positively influence the image you convey. Think of pleasant things to do, retain excitement in your voice, stay positive, and stay trim. I don't mean that women must be a size eight or ten, or men must have a thirty-two-inch waistline, but no matter your size, fight the bulges and lumps. Let me tell you that doing yoga, attending dance exercise classes, and walking daily—at least a mile—does wonders. I don't weigh much less than I did at forty, but I am taking in seams since I started a regular daily program of exercise. And I do feel peppy.

A number of accomplices can assist us in this personal quest. Hairdressers primp us with modish flips and swirls; yoga trainers prompt us to tune up; massage masters roll a little extra fat from the thighs. Our skin can have the glow we want, enhanced as skin is by the finest creams, which do shade out little wrinkles. Nutritionists busily devise tempting uses of veggies and fruits; there are times you have to chuckle over the fanciful presentations. Thus, being well put together, top to toe, inside and outside, you are primed for adventure, and your age is anyone's guess.

Do you gasp when you are told about someone reaching one hundred years of age? There were 92,127 persons 100 or older in 2008 (0.24 percent of the total 65-and-up population). This is a 147 percent increase from 1990 figure of 37,306.[2] Can we safely estimate one million at present?

Early this year, we celebrated the hundredth birthday of Manny Mandel. Because he had been financial advisor to the Footlighters, an organization of professional performers, they threw a party for him at the Miami Country Club. The festivities included dinner followed by professional entertainment. The officers of the club presented him with a gift of lifelong membership.

Manny smiled broadly, his blue eyes still a-twinkle, and asked, "Do you have enough money for that in your treasury?" His face was hardly wrinkled, except for laugh lines. He hadn't lost his spirit or his humor.

Extended age opens new passages never traversed before; new questions and solutions never considered before; and new modes of living never experienced before. And, as mentioned earlier, the old solutions don't resonate with older people.

Irving S. tells me that when he was widowed at age eighty-five, each of his two daughters offered their homes to him. His response: No thank you. He explained, "I will live independently as long as I am able and then, if need be, I'll go to an assisted-living residence. But living with my children is not an option for me. I love them both and know their love and concern is sincere, but I need to exercise my freedom to

---

2 Administration on Aging. US Department of Health and Human Services.

go where and with whom I wish without imposing on my children. I know they would not feel imposed upon. Theirs is honoring the elderly, protecting with love, but I don't want to be protected when I still feel like their protector or providing what they might like to enhance their homes; sometimes being able to do things for them is good for me. I am still capable and proud. And despite any protest, I know moving in with them would alter their way of life. Again, no thank you."

As for Abe K., he lived alone for five years, testing the extent of aloneness he could endure. "I failed the test. I'm happier being among people." He is content living in an Independent Living Center.

Many seniors' unwillingness to live with their children reflects a change of perspective. Additionally, many people entering their later years are more financially prepared than in the past. Pensions have made a difference. Investments seem secure, although many have taken a hit and have had to adjust their sights. Science has also contributed many innovations that keep them relatively healthy. These factors do contribute to a good frame of mind. Many have retained or developed a sense of humor.

Irving had two residences, one in New York and one in Florida. He was still enjoying New York life—the museums, adult classes, concerts, theater, and social and religious events—into his nineties. His children did prevail upon him to stop traveling back and forth. He gave up his apartment in New York and still regrets having done so.

Independence, however fleeting, is cherished. Many elders get their first taste of unwanted intrusion imposed on them by children who sell their car. Something like culture shock sets in. Their ability to live their lives responsibly is habitually questioned and tested. Their accounts and distribution of funds are challenged, tethered, altered. Some children become authorities presiding over their parents' expenditures: how they budget and pay their bills, not to mention how they eat, drink, sleep, and recreate. These children also fuss over Dad's or Mom's pills. A sense of distrust or judgment begins to affect older people, diluting their independence.

Can we ever change the mind-set of a public that believes older people are senile? My greatest peeve is with people who immediately question the memory or state of mind of seniors: "Are you sure you can't find it? Did you look in unlikely places, like the refrigerator?" "Do you really want to travel?" "It's so difficult for an older person ... why don't you get an aide?" Why?

Granted, many elderly become fragile, halting, and handicapped. These people may need special care, but forgetting a word or a name does not signify dementia, Alzheimer's, or any other ailment requiring supervision. Yes, older people are prone to a long list of debilitating ailments, but people have to comprehend that more than 50 million people over 65 are living in the United States this year, with a projected 20 percent increase expected in the next decade. About 11 percent (3.7 million) of older Medicare enrollees receive personal care from a paid or unpaid source. The rest are capable of meeting their own needs, and most want to live meaningful lives.

This huge, relatively healthy population, capable of spending their days and evenings in pleasant diversion, continue to search for and inevitably set guidelines for future generations of elders. *Gloom* and *doom* are not in their lexicon. Elders may move more slowly and with less energy, but they seek companionship for walks and trips around town, even travel abroad. They are capable of clear and profound thinking. Sumner is 102 years old and plays duplicate bridge with scoring a few times a week. He will invite a partner to dance during social events. Edith B., retired Captain, WACS, WWII, anticipates her 100th birthday in April 2012 with crackling humor, decorative barette in her hair and bounce in her walk.

There are many elders whom we admire and emulate. If they are fortunate enough to have their mates, they find greater safety and pleasure in their relationships. They are sharing and enjoying their togetherness, still holding hands—even if it's for balance—and feeling grateful that they've weathered rough seas and remained together. When they do look back at what disgruntled them in the office, what set them back in their careers, what caused them to stumble on the rough road of life, they can weigh those rough times against the good years, the advances made, the joy of bonus years, and the lessons they learned and shared. Most people come out ahead.

What is ahead for couples that have traveled the family and/or the career road? Change? Giving up big homes for smaller places with less upkeep and care? Seeking new places of interest they had no time for in their busy lives or knew only through post cards? They might visit a museum or scan brochures for courses they could take on subjects they never had a chance to pursue. An expanding horizon is before them.

Doing new and different things soon leads to considering more adventurous prospects, like moving to a new place. Wielding their asset of mobility, off they go to the Carolinas, Florida, California, Arizona, or any other state or country that entices them.

What about the many people who have lost or divorced mates? What are their choices? Some of the above, with even more options! There may be some doubt about how younger generations define future, but the definition among the single older generation is now. Now is when they need answers to their questions. Now is when they want to do things, go places, meet companionable people. Yes, you've come to a fork in the road: take the old way or try a new one? You may well remember the cryptic smarts of Yogi Berra: When you come to a fork in the road, take it!

Should you deny your past? Not at all! There's much value in the experiences you've acquired, much that has been sorted out and retained. It's called wisdom. The older generation keeps hoping that such wisdom will impact their younger ones, that subsequent generations will recognize how caring and perseverance can be relied upon when the road gets bumpy, that they will give their all in solving perplexities that arise instead of becoming dependent on counselors if and when the threat of divorce—or whatever spoils reasonable agreement—seeps into their relationships. Everyone lives with the unknown, is knocked around by the unknown, and learns the power of the unknown.

Esther C. Gropper

**To be able to look back upon one's life with satisfaction
is to enjoy it twice.**
e.c.g.

Questions We Need to Ask

At lunch with one of her friends, Bluma S. shared thoughts about a series of lectures she was to give on "The Golden Years: Are They So?" when her friend quickly replied, "For me, it was a loss. Not only loved ones, family, friends. Most of all of myself." The implications were clear. She mourned the loss of energy, faculties, people who played significant roles in her life, the conduct of her life. She showed the symptoms of what Bluma called the existentialism of despair. The challenge was to find replacements for the missing parts, recover, or even have some access to the will to keep trying. What was it I did that made me feel good in the past and accomplished? What didn't I do that could have enriched my life? Who and what made a difference? The people I wanted to be with, talk that is stimulating.

Bluma quietly asked, "Why aren't you gathering new and cheerful people around you? Haven't you observed people with handicaps who feel good about themselves, have a great sense of humor and are very creative?" (These very traits describe Bluma herself.)

At dinner that evening at the senior residence where we live, Bluma, still troubled by her friend's despondency, asked her dinner companions how they viewed life. Paula said, "I look at life as a bucket. You can fill it, fill half or you can keep it half empty."

That challenged me to ask Bruce R. about the way he viewed life. Without hesitation, he answered, "Well, I'd have to ask for two buckets." His remark revealed how richly experienced his life was and how well he enriched the lives of others.

We were to learn more about what made aging acceptable and

Esther C. Gropper

gracefully experienced for Bruce. And for others. We were well aware of people for whom aging was frightening, a span of uncertainty and loneliness that Heinrich Heine (19th century) said was the worst poison. What made the difference? How was one to alleviate the sadness? Why was the bucket empty for one and yet another person wanted two to carry the gifts of life? Was it all a matter of luck? Didn't most everyone have his share of sorrow and joy to carry through life? Kahlil Gibran, Persian poet, offered: Of life's two chief prizes, beauty and truth, I found the first in a loving heart and the second in a laborer's hand. Kahlil Gibran had the great sense of awe of life's bounty that we find in people like Bruce. Perhaps many humans aren't schooled to focus on the more inspiring lessons of our great forebears. Does it redound upon us to ask if there are more ways than one to measure the contents of our buckets?

How and when do we begin to fill the buckets? Bruce's childhood was in revolution torn Russia where Communist rule was ruthless on the capitalists. The Rabison family gathered together whatever possessions they could carry and became refugees on a long trail towards a haven. They were fortunate to arrive in the United States able to re-establish home and business. Flaming red haired Bruce received his education at the Yeshiva, a parochial school, and went on to receive his B.S. with exceptional honors at the Yeshiva University. The President of the Yeshiva University, Dr. Bernard Revel, called Dean of Harvard Law School, Dr. Jim Landis, to urge his acceptance of three graduates with exceptional accomplishments.

They were the very first Jewish students admitted to Harvard Law School. They set the precedent for the future. The Dean of Harvard Law School called Dr, Revel with this message: If ever you have students of their caliber, be sure to contact us.

All three students received their law degrees in 1937, at the height of the Depression. Law interns, generally, were hired without pay but with his credentials, Bruce received $5.00. per week. When he worked assiduously on the research and brief preparation for the success of a case that was awarded an unprecedented settlement and received nothing but a thanks for his intense efforts, Bruce decided law was not going to offer him a livelihood for many years nor the fulfillment of his hope to marry and support his lovely Evelyn. He met Evelyn when he boarded at her mother's home for room and kosher meals. She was fifteen years old when he came there. He watched this snippy adolescent grow in to a tall blonde beauty; she watched his finely etched face take on maturity. Physically, both developed aristocratic confident stature.

Bruce borrowed five thousand dollars and with a friend who shared equal investment went into the fabric weaving and printing business, a craft he observed and learned in his father's business. The fascinating story of his life involved investments on three continents where he built plants and produced native-design fabrics. He met the illustrious heads of many states, learned to speak many languages. In fact, when he gave his military service to the U.S., during World War II, he learned that the government was searching for Japanese speaking soldiers. Of the many languages he spoke, Japanese was not among them but Bruce ventured to tell his superior officers that he was lingual in Russian. He thought they could use his agility but they, in their wisdom, recognized the resourcefulness. They did send him to learn Japanese. He became proficient in it and along with the many languages he already knew, he was a great asset to his adopted land.

Bruce is a truly humanitarian Renaissance man and a privilege to know. And how remarkable it is that, despite loss of Evelyn and a cancer stricken daughter Sue, his own failing health, that he can still look back on his life with satisfaction. He still greets visitors with a contagious smile.

We can all share stories of 'larger-than-life' personalities and they always seem to amaze us but in our wisdom, we also ask about the minutia of life. How do they, the great and the average, handle the prickling questions that affect dispositions and public personalities? If we are happy with ourselves and/or accept ourselves, we are happier people. How do we attain that attitude? Why not give the small things some attention? Little things add up to something bigger; they add up to happier people. There is no reason for not dressing up the face or figure if that contributes to a desired demeanor. How can minor attentions to ourselves make us feel good about ourselves? Let's address some of those perplexities.

Do you frown at the wrinkles around your eyes, your lips? Did you ever stop to think that every wrinkle has a story in your life? Try keeping a notebook on the subject. You may even find that in retrospect, you see incidents with humor. Your family will enjoy your life story. And when you smile, the wrinkles are pressed out. Women! Creams fill out those lines.

Do you weigh too much? Have I touched a hot button? Start now on exercise and diet regimens. Hint: Smaller portions. Longer walks.

Are you too short? Shoe designers have you in mind these days. Too tall? Can there be such a thing? Those nifty flats—short for "flattering"—do something for you.

Not sure what colors or designer lines are best for you? Why be afraid of color? Nature isn't. Nor do you ever see flowers too large for their stalks, but large flowers and pleats emphasize size; straight lines or A-lines are more becoming. Longitudinal or elongated lines create height; horizontal lines cut figures and give the illusion of shorter figures.

What about the emotions that tug at your heart?

Can't combat loneliness? What's the opposite? Clusters of people? Where do they gather? Why aren't you in their midst?

How do you react to setbacks? A broken relationship? Rejection? Professional disappointment?

Do you recognize a controlling person? Baiting remarks?

Do you build up defenses that defeat you? Lies? Silences?

Do you share your feelings?

Is it hard to repair friendship after a quarrel or breakup? Do you seriously want to?

Can you resolve why you quarreled?

Dance until the Music Stops

Do you know any clever ways to initiate conversation ... that lead to dates?

Are the arrows finding their targets?

Consider these questions as you peruse the chapters to follow. Keep in mind that our generations (those in their seventies, eighties, and nineties) are facing old and new problems that take aim at successful aging. Be sure to keep some arrows in reserve to use as you tackle the unknown ahead.

Esther C. Gropper

Age, I make light of it,
Fear not the sight of it.
Time's but a playmate
Whose toys are divine.
e.c.g.

Life as an Investment Folio

Bluma confronts audiences with questions about satisfied lives, but that seems to evoke unresolved dilemmas. At one of her discussions, she invited her audience to look at their lives as investment portfolios, as profits and losses. Included in their lists were personal losses in health: eyesight, hearing, word and name recall, short-circuited thoughts and difficult decisions, diminished mobility—a bleak outlook for the future. The loss of one's self is the biggest loss. Another ventured, "I am told about diminution of skills, dexterity, and potency. I am waiting to be told how to balance that aspect of the portfolio."

Perhaps by considering the gains. One man said, "As for gains, being more compassionate, more gentle in our relationships, friendships in new places and new activities." The response took on a different tone when another admitted, "Things I didn't know I could do or would venture to do or find time to do."

In summary, we need to find our own inner strength to pull ourselves up by our own bootstraps. We need to lighten the baggage we take as we travel on. It is time to stop carrying old hurts that weigh us down and keep nagging for attention—time to stop rehearsing arguments for quarrels that are long past. We must give eviction notices to past disappointments lodged in our minds. We should clear out old, out-of-style stuff to make space for other ways to make life better. All the misused energy is best applied to creative living that lingers with lighter baggage and brighter moments. Everything is choice.

Bluma asked which was the greater factor: loss or gain? One answer was, "If we are talking in market metaphors, there are the conservative investors, who sought a moderate, quiet life, and others who took risks for good or bad, taking new mates or engaging in new ventures, who retained that attitude as they aged. There was excitement and possibility—not a lion-hearted demeanor, but courtly."

Further comments showed, in some, a common inclination toward caution, even being overly cautious, with residues of "What would happen if I had dared to …" Views certainly illustrated the unique nature of the baggage we carry into aging. The conclusion seemed to be that their loss was greater than their gain. Well, what about the gains? Are you proud of what you accomplished? Why not convey the attributes you bring to your present status, showing them off?

Next, Bluma recommended that participants set a brighter course of action, or at least think about untapped possibilities for a more promising future. What, for them, was the meaning of life? What could they share with their children, their grandchildren? What was important to them? What had they accomplished? Bluma asked how participants could rechannel their emotions, or convert their worries, anxieties, anger—the negative aspects of their lives—into something more positive, something that gives meaning to life. If the focus of their lives had been sports, for instance, and there were now restrictions, how could they perpetuate the exhilaration they had once felt?

Conversation took a different turn when one participant admitted, "I didn't know I could imbue my six-year-old grandson with a love of golf until I took him to a golf range, where he followed my example and hit the ball a hundred yards. He's fourteen now, and we have a great sport to share."

Doesn't that apply to everyone? My companion once had a rich baritone voice. He told me that he sang his children to sleep every night. They stayed awake in their beds, waiting for his late return from his store. Now he grieves for the losses of two children and a wife. He falters when he starts to sing. He tried but gave up the choral group. He was told he'd have to forgo things in aging. With his ready sense of humor, he mused that he had always liked wine, women, and song. He gave up song.

After sharing a laugh—a good way to sidestep plaintiveness—we continued talking about one of the most serious challenges to good moods.

"Everything we've mentioned," Esther pointed out, "happens to younger people as well."

In advanced age, a stumbling on the tennis court or an awkward move in golf can result in a bone fracture and months of recuperation. Your body will tell you if and when it resents strenuous sports in later years. What can you do then that still has the elements of sports to it, that lightens the depression at any time of life—besides being a spectator from the couch or going out to watch a game?

Expectations vary for each sex. The lesson to take from senior players is that it's wise to lower expectations and play for pleasure, not competitiveness. Ninety-year-olds in our residence go out on Saturday mornings and just hit balls to each other. They can get a mechanical ball-thrower paced for their abilities or visit putting greens that still keep the juices flowing. There are even the occasional visits with grandchildren when they share stance, movements, expertise, making a happy moment and memory! They are being physical, useful, needed—achievers from whom not everything has been taken away.

When you start thinking, other activities come to mind: billiards, table tennis, long walks getting acquainted with nature. Look around, and you might find little preserved areas that are alive with other forms of life—coves and caves you never had a chance to explore. You may reach a plateau. Take a deep breath and then continue your exploration of new interests.

Esther C. Gropper

**Love reads the literature of another's being.
When your affection is kindled,
the world of the intellect takes on a new tenderness and
compassion.
Bob**

We Are Living a New Kind of Tribal Life

We are living a new kind of tribal life: one that is age-oriented. We are taking along old elements that probably worked for us and are intrinsic to orderly living: daily toiletry routines, tidy dressing, healthy food habits, walking and/or exercising five times a week, and so on. If you already possess companionship techniques that help create new friendships in a new environment, you can expand viable activities and seek out and explore new possibilities compatible with age, all while allowing the private time that's important for self-searching and reaffirming good qualities in yourself and new acquaintances.

On May 22, 2009, the *New York Times* ran a story about a retirement community. The reporter, Benedict Carey, had sought answers from residents about longevity, their activities, and their general outlook. Carey's focus centered on the bridge game that was habitual there but offered benefits that could have been gained from any activity that engrosses the mind. Dr. Claudia Kawass of University of California, Irvine, called these residents the most successful agers on earth who are just beginning to teach us what's important in their genes, in their routine, and in their lives. She gave this succinct insight: it's very important to use your brain, to keep challenging the mind. But she did not claim that all activities are equal. We are seeing some evidence that a social component may be crucial.

I was particularly impressed with the conclusive commentary on social context. It reminded me of a moment when I suggested to one of our residents who didn't play cards that he, a former engineer, try Sudoku, the math puzzle with which many people seem engrossed. He looked at me and simply stated, "Not for me. My work was solitary. I want to be with people now."

Was this an excuse to reject the idea? I had offered several ways to stay occupied without depending on other people to satisfy his needs. Such struggles were often the case with nonjoiners. Somehow, I was off track with him. I prompted him to express his interests, but he fumbled in his efforts to find the words.

That was when I was informed of Dr. Maurer's book *One Small Step Can Change Your Life: The Kaizen Way*. I stubbed my brain on his reference to a patient who rejected solitary activities, saying, "There's nothing sociable about it." Think about it. Sociability contributes greatly towards to contentment among the aging. It is the antithesis of loneliness.

I found that I shared a basic curiosity with Dr. Maurer: I have also been intrigued by the opposite of failure. When a dieter loses ten pounds and keeps it off, I want to know how. If a person finds love after years of unsatisfying relationships, I'm curious about the strategies that made happiness possible. When a corporation stays on top of its game for fifty years, I want to understand the decisions behind the success.

I raise similar questions about human relationships and human traits that serve us well to develop. We all encounter stumbling blocks and forks in the road. I learned to pause, especially after an unhappy sequence, to ask myself what I may have done badly, what I should learn to avoid. In retrospect, I would identify warning signs I had ignored: His needs came first. His love was on time-shared schedules. His demands supplanted my need for tenderness and solicitate. Why I had continued a relationship that held little satisfaction was one of the hardest questions to probe and answer for myself. I hungered for love and self-esteem (a need rooted in early childhood that had awakened from its slumber) but I conveyed that by giving attention to his desires—hoping, I guess, that he would reciprocate. I had to learn there's no magic to wishing. There's no mind reading. You have to say what you want, and it should come as no surprise to the other to hear it. He should want it for you, just as if you truly wanted it for him, and vice versa. When I saw that and finally admitted it to myself, I suffered through changes. I could never be happy with a self-centered person who looked at his partner as a product he had a taste for when the desire arose, without ever considering the counter-desires facing him. I suffered through changes in myself as I moved on, became more discerning, and found myself rewarded with both love and self-esteem. Ironically, our deepest needs hold us back from fulfilled lives. My mother-in-law used to say, "An empty apartment is better than a bad tenant." At Harvard Business College, they say, "It is much more efficient to leave a position empty than to fill it with the wrong person."

Esther C. Gropper

**Lend me your life;
Lend me your heart
Replete with thankfulness.
—William Shakespeare,** *King Henry VI*

Taking Personal Inventory

Bluma pursued this topic in her next session: "What's on Your Mind?" The stage was set for participants to ponder the meaning of their lives.

What is important to you? How do you look at your accomplishments? How do you think your children and grandchildren see you? How do you feel about your relationships?

Taking personal inventory should be an ongoing process. Get familiar with your attributes.

These are honest questions to ask yourself.

Apparently, the questions needed refinement, because one person answered that his relationships were with academic, career, and social contacts, and each showed a different aspect of himself.

Certainly, but cumulatively? Are you the sum total of all of your relationships? If so, how are you using your self-acquired experiences at your retirement stage? Are you using that knowledge in some way now? Are you helping others? Do you still want something more for yourself? Do you have plans for that something more?

While you still have the promise of years ahead at your disposal, what do you need to do to fill those years pleasantly? To this question came a hostile response: "Why do you assume that we're all able to do the things we want to do?"

"Fair enough question, and an ironic one," responded the moderator from her wheelchair. "But I'm going to ask you how you can rechannel your worries, anxieties, concerns, and anger—the negative aspects of your lives—to something more positive that reflects on your meaning of life."

"I like sports," one man attested, "and now a lame leg keeps me from the sports I love."

"Today, at three, is the US Open's main event, the men's championship," came the quick response. "True, you are a spectator, which you were even in the past, but you can still get exhilaration from watching. And if you can still hit a ball, come out to the court for some practice and amiability. Or, do a few rounds on the putting greens."

Another participant added, "There's a lesson to take from senior players of tournaments. They lower their expectations and play for the pleasure, and a modicum of competitiveness. Countywide programs are offered in the parks. Ninety-year olds get out Saturday mornings and just enjoy hitting balls to each other. Other communities have a mechanical ball thrower paced for lower expectations. Putting greens can still keep the juices flowing. There are the occasional visits with grandchildren when you can share stance movements, expertise … happy moments and memories in virtual reality. You are physical, useful, needed, enjoyed—an achiever who still has something to offer.

When you start thinking, other activities come to mind: billiards, tennis, getting acquainted with nature on long walks, seeing preserved areas that are alive with other forms of life, a chance to explore outer banks and low mountain trails.

Bluma led the discussion back to the investment portfolio. "On the plus side, in our later years, we have more patience, not only with others but with ourselves. We have only to look at ourselves. I am in a wheelchair; Esther recently abandoned her walker. What is your level of patience?"

A tremendous expansion of patience was acknowledged. I started to reflect on how my own patience developed. I had been a teacher of lively adolescents in a schoolroom with windows overlooking the football field. I had to know how to maintain attention to my lesson. I learned a great deal about determination, about not giving up because of competition outdoors. And I adapted, writing spelling lessons that included *laceration, indefatigable, debacle, skirmish, vanquished,* and so on—words they could use in describing football plays in one short paragraph. When they spoke, I wrote on the board *spoke,* and then I deliberately dropped the *e* and put in an extra *o* to make it *spook,* or some such exercise of word variation or meaning. Did it work? Most of the time. Did students learn vocabulary and the value of correct spelling? Was it a way to prepare for SATs? Yes!

Patience and determination: they help in any profession, in every stage of life. And keep in mind that inspiration comes with every heartbeat. You have only to tune in.

When Bluma spoke of adjusting to changes, I was reminded of the heavy plate I had carried as a widow,. Attracting and making new friends (male or female), playing the dating game, and courting—it all took me back to my teens in some ways and was utterly embarrassing at first. Unearthed emotions and behavior I had thought long past taunted me. Many seniors experience similar feelings.

Perhaps for me, strong changes in my life made me redirect my energies. One son was in college; the other was serving in the Navy. (We were at war in Vietnam.) My daughter was in high school. I was a single mother with children looking to her for strength and guidance. Talk about new emotions, coping, and sustaining a family!

I was in a secure teaching position. I resigned from my work at the zenith of my career to marry and join Barney in a Florida retirement community. I was completely out of my element there, living among sedentary people whose vision of senior age was life in a rocking chair. Florida was intellectually barren at the time. There I was, in alien territory, away from family and friends, having left my occupation and married somebody relatively new in my life—more changes than a reasonable person should make at any time. I should have known that. I had had years of experience as a guidance counselor that I now applied to myself as I examined alternative possibilities and capabilities in a plus-and-minus diagram. I would recommend this process for anyone about to consider changes, especially men and women whose age is against them when seeking employment—not an uncommon complaint, even among men and women seeking the coupled life.

What strengths and interests in life could I use in another situation? What were my assets and liabilities?

What came to mind immediately was that I never had enough time to write. I really found a way to fill my days in later life as long as my mind and hands were healthy. I also thought about long-lasting abilities that people have, such as musical training; musicians or vocalists have a lifelong talent that can sustain them at any stage of their lives. Many community religious or senior centers have choral or small instrumental groups that provide entertainment as well as gratification for the participants. Crafts and arts are good activities for the retiree. Look at the inspiring exhibits in museums, colleges, and civic centers; these displays include drawings, watercolor or acrylic paintings, photography, woodworking, and sculpting. Why not try your hand at one or another activity? Do you think we've run the gamut?

In this list, I should include the stage background paintings that are made for each holiday or seasonal change. Pinky Fairchild, in our residence, is particularly imaginative and creative in her renditions. I think that sources of talent, experience, and creative ability abide in many senior communities, and if one organizational leader arises, many flock to join.

This returns us to the original question: what can you do? What would you like to do? Which activity have you never dared to explore? What have you done that gives you inspiration for what you can do in your senior years? I might add group living or club participation can build inspiration, confidence, trust, and comfort. You can't measure that, but it is one of the surprises of senior life.

Another question: what can't you do for lack of materials, tools, space? I am thinking of Bob, who wants to write a melody for a poem I wrote but doesn't have a piano available to him. In this case, a keyboard is the answer if he can afford it.

In a brainstorming session, residents named the following activities we see going on, just off the cuff: knitting shawls and booties for hospital patients, making bead jewelry for charity sales or personal accessories, taking pictures, writing. Active groups create stories and memoirs that are shared and often show up in print or little plays. Scrapbooks have become highly professional through help from stores now specializing in products for this interest. What a way to sort out pictures and letters that you want to share with posterity! Cards and letters we make describe places and recall memorable experiences.

We know people whom we wouldn't want to change—not one hair on their heads. But what do we do about the chronic complainers? Is the concentrated social company of elders conducive to criticisms of food, environment, and attire, or have such detractors always been contemptuous? Does aging only make you more so? Do you have to invite a qualified social worker to come with exercises and plans to reach pleasurable aging, to help you reach your inner store of knowledge that leads to a better image of yourself? Take inventory of yourself. I'm sure you will find how much you have learned about life that would be useful to you now. If you are so overpowered by grief that you feel immobile or marginalized, seek counsel. There's more to life that you are entitled to. You can gain insight into yourself and others. Read a book like *The Mature Mind*, by Dr. G. D. Cohen, who says that with age, you can examine life, achieve peace of mind, and attain a sense of completion and self-fulfillment—the sweet fruits of aging!

I've achieved that sweet peace of mind. Despite The Depression hardships, I attended evening college classes. I attained degrees that led to teaching, counseling and writing. With my objectives well defined, I was able to handle widowhood with three children. I provided for their education. I emphasized the importance of independence, another way of saying self-reliance.

Esther C. Gropper

You dance, she admonished, with two left feet.
You're wrong my dear heart;
I dance with two right feet.
—   Bob.

Meeting and Greeting

As suggested in a workshop in which the facilitator was indicating how to rephrase questions to get more positive responses, I told the group that if you ask an elderly person, "How are you feeling?" you are sure to get a litany of aches, pains, medications, and so on. But if you say, "You are wearing a pretty scarf," you are apt to get a smile and a thank-you. If you ask someone like Bob, "How's the world treating you?" you're apt to get an answer like, "Sometimes like a dog; sometimes like a hydrant," with a hint of boyish teasing spreading across his face.

There is an art, a grace in meeting people. It's a learned skill. Physical therapist Patrice knows that asking aging people (from around fifty years old and up) how they feel leads to a litany of ailments. Thus, she illustrated with one patient: "Well, Stanley, did you move any mountains today?" By his puzzled expression and his blundering answer ("Eh? What did you say?"), he indicated a hearing loss. She asked it louder: "Have you moved any mountains?"

"Oh," he responded, "I thought you asked me if I moved my bowels!" Laughter is the note on which the therapy started.

Laughter is the key to a lighter heart. One resident at a senior center who has a collection of films told me that when he feels the cloud of depression descending, he puts on an "I Love Lucy" or Bill Cosby tape to bypass a bad mood.

That's one technique to employ to lighten the mood. If residing in a lively community is the answer to a more fulfilled life, why is depression a common complaint? One cause Bluma offered was that mingling with depressing people—people who start, continue, and conclude every exchange with their own problems—can cause one to become depressed as well. Some residents will even greet you with a litany of their ailments—what we call an organ recital.

Getting back to Patrice's technique, start with "That's an attractive scarf or string of beads or hat," or "Myrna gave a great lecture today about strange conclusions to court cases," or give any positive greeting. It makes a big difference.

Playing the "I Used to …" game can be fun and funny; ask residents to provide answers in twenty-five words or less. On an invitation to play tennis: "I used to be a great tennis player." My aged father-in-law answered, "I used to … went to war." (That was WWII). Sparked by that comment, Bob said, "I used to have hair; now I have hairs."

One neighbor said of another, "She is approaching a hundred and still stands as straight as an arrow." To which four-foot-ten Paula answered, "And now I stand as straight as a bow." In these days of rising costs, Mort bemoaned the future prospects: "I used to be an affluent man; now I worry about managing my bills."

Some of life's gifts can only be acquired with age: wisdom, mastery in hundreds of different spheres of study that require decades of learning. Growing old can be filled with positive experiences; successful aging means harnessing and manifesting the enormous positive potential that each one of us has for growth, love, and happiness.

This potential for pleasing ourselves doesn't pop up in later life. It starts with our early responses, with seeing new faces and hearing new voices. The art of meeting and greeting people starts in the cradle with a sense of how parents respond to a baby's cry, and whether they greet or coddle their baby just for the love of it. You can determine a child's confidence at the playground. He will gravitate toward a group in play and somehow find acceptance through a smile, a bodily gesture, a trusting look in the eye, or another signal that children readily read. Similarly, a bully or brat is rejected after some signal of aggression.

I recall an early incident in my life when visiting cousins. My father bought a gift for us to play with in the garden: a set of garden tools that consisted of a shovel, a rake, a hoe, and packets of flower seeds. There were three tools, and we were three children happily involved in planning our cousins' garden. Along came another boy who asked to play.

"We have no tools for you," one of us answered. "You can't play." He turned brusquely away but returned a few minutes later with a coal shovel, obviously a menacing tool.

"You can't play here with that big shovel," I said authoritatively. With that he lifted the shovel as a weapon and hit me on the head. Yes, blood gushed. My aunt got hysterical, but a neighbor carried me to the drugstore, where a doctor was reached to stitch up the gash. You can probably read the emotions of the children involved, but the inability to control anger and the tendency to misuse aggression is troublesome. We learn as we grow, under reliable guidance, to understand extremes, to check distressing emotions, to find defenses that help us maintain stability, and to choose companions and activities that are right for us. Those who don't are shunned and become socially inept. An accepted adage that sums this up is "We learn from what we like and from what we dislike." Sometimes we're surprised at the way we store those lessons.

Another experience in my young life, growing up on a farm, was attending an authentic little red schoolhouse. Sixteen children of age six to twelve in one classroom with one teacher received fine schooling in the three R's. The teacher went from one child to another, teaching levels of arithmetic appropriate to each child's age and ability, giving an assignment, moving to the next child, and so on. Then followed a round of spelling and writing. We worked through all categories of study without a sound in the room. When you finished your assigned work, you were to go quietly to the shelves for a book to read, which would be related to social studies. At recess, we had farm-fresh milk and snacks. After lunch, all played softball, with even rankings chosen for both sides. This was the best school experience I had. I don't recall fistfights or dirty words. I came to the city school far ahead of my categorical class.

And just to review from above with a note of caution: our brains may often have very little control over *when* we are swept with emotion, nor over *what* emotion it will be. But we can have some say in *how long* an emotion will last. The issue arises not with garden-variety sadness, worry, or anger; normally such moods pass with time and patience. But when these emotions are of great intensity and linger past an appropriate point, they shade over into their distressing extremes: chronic anxiety, uncontrollable rage, depression. At their most severe and intractable, they may only be lifted with medication, psychotherapy, or both.[3]

Anger is energizing, even exhilarating ... but anger's seductive, persuasive power can be controlled. Some counselors maintain that venting anger is catharsis, but that suggestion does not address your ability to reason through anger—to solve problems cogently despite your emotions.

By the time we are adults, and surely by retirement age, we have social skills that work for us. The atmosphere can be very social and accepting. We become more considerate; we become skilled in organizing or seeking out players for our particular games; we've learned to prevent conflicts (or when they arise, to use diplomacy to calm the air); we know to excuse ourselves from ripening flare-ups or turn the talk around to something less irritating. We all recognize and seek out the people with polished manners who offer charming, witty, and bright conversation. We create our own harmonious environment.

---

3 I am giving you points from Dr. D. Goleman's book, Emotional Intelligence.

Esther C. Gropper

Forgiveness is the scent of the violet
on the boot that crushed it.

—Mark Twain

Finding New Interests

Florida was intellectually barren in 1975, when I moved there. I was, in alien territory, away from family and friends, having left my occupation and married somebody relatively new in my life—more changes than a reasonable person should make at any time. I should have known that. I had had years of experience as a guidance counselor that I now applied to myself, examining alternate possibilities in two columns: plus and minus. I would recommend this process to anyone about to consider changes, not the least of which would be men and women whose age would work against them when seeking employment, not an uncommon complaint.

What were my strengths and main interests in life that I could explore in any given situation? This process was similar to Bluma's recommended analysis of assets and liabilities. What came to mind immediately was that I never had enough time to write. I really found a way to fill my days in later life as long as my mind and hands were healthy. When you fully commit to an idea, nature and life conspire to actualize it.

I am also thinking about long-lasting abilities that people have, such as musical training, whether instrumental or vocal. Many community religious or senior centers have choral or small instrumental groups that provide entertainment as well as gratification for the participants. Crafts and arts are good activities for the retiree. Look at the exhibits we have here monthly: drawings, watercolor and acrylic paintings, photography, woodworking, and sculpting. Why, I think we've run the gamut.

Bluma couldn' wait to remind us of the talent shows staged twice a year by residents Horty, Helen and Selma showcasing original skits, lyrics and costuming. I think," she added, "that sources of talent, experience, and creative ability abide in many senior communities, and if one organizational leader arises, many flock to join."

This leads back to our original question: What can you do? What would you like to do that you never had time to, or dared to, explore? What have you done that gives you inspiration for what you can do in your senior years? I might add that group living and club participation build trust and comfort. You can't measure that, but it is one of the surprises of senior life.

Bluma and I continued to brainstorm, just naming activities off the cuff: knitting shawls and booties for hospital patients, making bead jewelry for charity sales or personal accessories, taking pictures, and writing. Active groups create stories and memoirs that are shared and often show up in print. Scrapbooks have become highly professional through help from stores now specializing in products for this interest. What a way to sort out pictures and letters that you want to share with posterity! Cards and letters made by residents describe places visited and memorable experiences.

"I had that sort of experience," Bluma said. "When I came home from surgery, I sorted cards, messages, and recipes." This led to talk about whom and where they were from, when they had arrived, and what they conveyed.

"I remember," Esther added, "when we visited my brother-in-law in Atlanta. We wanted to see the new Hyatt Hotel. They had the first bubble elevator. We were the first guests in the rooftop restaurant. When the maître d' discovered we were from New York and this was our first visit to Atlanta, he gave us the royal treatment. Pictures were taken that appeared in the Atlanta newspaper with recipes of food prepared for us. My ten-year-old daughter had her first op-ed exposure."

"That's something for a scrapbook," Bluma answered. "*Special Events in My Life*." At that moment, a group of volunteers came into the room to design flower arrangements for the dining tables. One lady was quick to acknowledge that this was her favorite weekly activity, one everyone could enjoy. The group decorated tables and halls for every holiday and event.

The nice part is that people work together on these projects. I believe every civic center and house of worship sponsors decorative arts, crafts, houseplant care, and so on. Join in. Make yourself a reward for the bravery, daring, and spunk with which you faced life and awaken the talent you have for new challenges. Need I remind readers again and again that ours is a precious gift of longer life with no forged pathways or guides from former generations? For those generations, sixty was old and the limit to life. Given three more decades, how will you spend them? Start your map for the journey ahead!

Acknowledge the hard realities of aging (there will be some) while at the same time celebrating the pleasurable times, the rewards. Concentrate on rewards meant only for you and proudly showcase your sculptures, beads, buttons, and bows. And fear not the degenerative reports you hear, because counterbalancing loss is the gain of the other side of your brain, which is activated as you get older—the one that was sleeping through most of life. Nudge it awake. Make it work for you. It's part of you. Exercise that gray matter with puzzles and games. Bridge, Scrabble, or any word or number game can help. Think back to the ways you helped your children and grandchildren develop intellectually and creatively. Now do it for yourself!

Esther C. Gropper

**Unwelcome Habits of the Past:
"She's late as usual. It takes her two hours to watch 60 Minutes!"
Tardiness: Not worth arguing about
when a sense of humor clears the air.
Bob.**

Art of Conversation

The art of conversation starts with humor.

Be alert to people around you. Look for quirks and kinks; read facial and body movements; take note of appearance and characteristics. Be generous with praise and appraisal.

Rosella paused at our table to say hello.

"You look terrific. You look as if you're dressed for a hot date," quipped one diner.

"No, but I'm ready for it when it comes."

That resulted in a laugh and set the tone for conversation during the meal.

Jesting about sex will always bring a laugh or a chuckle. It need not be smutty or crude. Amy Campbell's framed needlepoint quote is a good example: "If you can't be fun in bed, at least be funny."

Good quips can be heard in most every conversation—not necessarily of the same ilk, but generally likely to reveal the good nature of someone with whom you'd like to share more time. Never having dined with Norma Hugo, I was enjoying her company more than in a bridge game. I listened as she talked about her eighty-seven years of life, during which she had survived three cancer operations. She could survey her life's activities and still say, "Anything worth doing is worth fighting for." Life, for her, was worth fighting for: "I put happiness into everything I do." And she has also looked for ways to bring happiness into other people's lives. She was a hospital volunteer for many years, during which time she brought a group of children in periodically for Show and Tell to cheer the patients. The girls wore nurse's caps; the boys carried stethoscopes. (I know, some of the girls should be carrying stethoscopes as well, and some of the boys should be wearing nurse's caps. Time marches on.) The children carried mechanical dolls and mimicked hospital routine.

At one time, when Norma lived in an adult community, she joined the hospitality committee. She greeted newcomers, sent lunch up to them during their unpacking days, and invited them to join others for dinner. The unique aspect of her program was that each committee member took a turn at inviting new residents to join other people. In a very short time, newcomers made acquaintances and arranged to be with each other in activities. Now at the senior residence, Norma is always in touch with others. She finds new interests and finds time to be of help to others as she is to Elmer, 100, whom she drives to the market for necessities.

While the most delightful personalities are revealed in humorous comments, the depth of an individual is in what he or she reveals about herself or himself. In a serious conversation about their different attitudes toward loss, men confessed they are more inclined to seek out a companion than are women. They described sleepless nights because they missed the warm proximity of a mate. Women, when free from a mate, sought something for themselves, some gratification long delayed because they had spent years taking care of everyone's needs. One lady turned down an arrangement, saying, "There's no room in either apartment for our combined medications. It would look more like a pharmacy than a love nest."

What do people want to talk about in later years? As you will note from the above, they speak of their unforgettable moments, their thoughts about the future, topical events—just about anything that keeps them au courant.

What enhances many conversations? Anecdotes. One conversation centered on pranks. Bob S. told of his college days. Then, as now, students bought used books. One student found that in his book, there was a reference in one chapter noting that the professor would, at this point, tell his story about the Irish army. Anticipating that tale, the students attended class to find that the professor was late. After waiting ten minutes, they left the classroom. The next day, they were berated for not waiting. "When you see my hat," he said, "I am here. You will wait." The following session, the one when the anecdote would be told, the professor, late as usual, walked in to find a hat on every student's seat. The professor had a sense of humor in more ways than indicated; he forgave them. Nor did he forget to tell them the anecdote.

Professor Schwarz, Austrian-born and still showing the brush of dialect, shared his worst moment: He informed a new class in philosophy that they might have a daily quiz if he found students unprepared to engage in discussion. Three days later, to make his point, he announced a quiz. Moans and groans erupted. The next day, class began similarly.

"What," he joshed, "you don't like my quizzies? Then wait. You will love my testees!" Realizing his unintended faux pas, he tried to hide his beet-red face but couldn't hide his chuckling body. Nothing to fear! His adult students applauded, and one even dared to say, "Who's afraid of the big bad quizzy? Who's afraid of the pestee testee?"

And as for jokes, which he always has ready, he tells of two refugees, greeting each other after a long interval and eager to show their facility with the English language.

"How is your wife? Any children?"

"My wife is unbearable."

"Are you sure that's the right word? Do you mean inconceivable?"

"No. I mean impregnable."

I cannot leave the topic of conversation without adding that one friend, not a great conversationalist herself, knew how to stimulate talk. In social settings – lunch, dinner, teas, any social gathering- she filled a void quickly with a topic for discussion. Her secret? She scoured the morning newspaper and made a mental catalog of topical matters. If it were today, she'd ask what the chances were of education focusing on learning and not on tests? Or middle east peace? Or who would be the best Republican candidate to beat Obama?

Esther C. Gropper

It is through social conversation that we learn about the people with whom we are friendly, learn what has made them the people they are.

Professor Robert Schwarz's childhood in Austria became a terrifying time when he watched the Nazi troops invade his county and issue its death warrants for his people. First came the humiliating experience of eviction from school, and then threats to his family. His father was taken to a concentration camp (despite his service in the army in World War I). Fearful of the lives of the two boys, Robert's parents managed to have him taken to England on the Kinder Transport train. Years later, he was able to join his family in Atlanta, Georgia. Both siblings are credits to our nation: Robert (Bob) is a professor of philosophy, and Fred is a professor of English.

Professor Fred Schwarz, visiting here, regaled us with stories of his youth. What he didn't tell us, Bob filled in. Fred was able to leave Austria with his parents, and he did remarkably well with his elementary-school English, eventually graduating from high school as valedictorian. Both Bob and Fred, reunited, attended Emory University. Fred's education was interrupted by the war. In the service, his talent for languages was noted, and he was assigned to study Japanese. He looked forward to an assignment as translator or interrogator, but the Army, in its inconsistency, assigned him to a detail in Texas guarding German prisoners.

When Fred returned four years later, he went back to Emory University. In this college, steeped in Confederate history and lore, the professor addressed him as *Colonel*, according him an unusual honor. Then the time came for researching some aspect of American history. Fred chose to write about Abraham Lincoln. Uh-oh! Ouch! Fred received a high grade for his essay, but from that day on, he was called Captain. Fred learned an unexpected lesson in Southern politics.

I often wonder if bickering is included in the category of conversation. Nothing is more embarrassing than being caught in the company of a bickering couple:

"You missed the turnoff."

"I'm not going that way."

"But that's the shortest way. You're always so stubborn, and then you get lost!"

"Do I always get you there?"

"Oh, why do I let you drive?"

"Because I still see and hear."

"A mixed blessing!"

And so all are subjected to a long record of their jibs and jabs.

When we mentioned this behavior at dinner one evening, Mort jested, "Next time I'm not going to marry a lawyer. They're always in court ... and not as the defender!"

To that, his lawyer wife adjured, "Marriage is grand. Divorce is a hundred grand." To which I add, humor should be your first choice in any conversation with spouse or friends. You will find humor interlaced in practically every aspect of this book. If any trait has served and preserved seniors, it is sharp wit. Perhaps I'm a sucker for a man or woman with a keen sense of humor. If life has taught me anything, it is that humor is the antidote for sadness. And while science can define longevity according to certainties like genes, environment, I have my own ingredient, my own spice: a sense of humor. That characteristic enables me to shed tensions.

I have a friend who has the happy faculty of flipping comments to the underside of things. Try a Salvador Dali with words. She does. Each phone conversation ends with a laugh. Just today, in a phone conversation with my loquacious friend Pearl, she urged me to give her my honest response to a dispute she and her daughter were having. It concerned her requested inscription on the headstone of her tomb: **What remains is the silent sound of memories.**

I was silently stunned by the poetry of the words. It reminded me of the quote you will find on page 174 by George Eliot, the last line of which is **The realm of silence is large beyond the grave.** I could only applaud the choice of epitaph. My loquacious friend, in a paradox to her nature, retained her wit and her exuberance of life. You will appreciate the visible garment of this gal when she added, "On the footstone, I want inscribed *Live and Be Well.*"

At this moment, my thoughts went back to a masquerade party we both attended, dressed as Not Knowing Which Side Is Up. Pearl wore panty hose over her head, shoes on her hands, a bikini worn upside down with rings and bracelets dangling below. I was her kid sister who dressed haphazardly, the way kids will do, with painted tattoos, feathers sticking to bubblegum in every unwanted place, and so on. You get the idea. Do something absurd (where it's safe to do so!) and life gets less serious ... and more fun.

Consider viewing unwelcome predicaments from the opposite perspective or from someone else's and you may reveal the true dimensions or absurdity of your feelings; it will open a path to new insights and relationships. Best of all, laugh at yourself as well as at others. In short, avoid taking yourself too seriously or taking others seriously to the extreme.

Esther C. Gropper

The absurdity of age is that older people say things in jest which are utterly true.
—Oscar Wilde

Things You Can Learn from a Donkey

A friend, Herb H., related this experience of when he visited a senior residence. Because of the many buildings and connecting halls, he wandered around with no sense of where the exit was. When he reached the desk of the concierge, he couldn't help saying to her, "You sure do make it hard to find your way out of here."

She laughed and answered in kind, "That's how we get new residents."

When I read about Rosamond Bernier (Metropolitan Museum of Art), she was retiring at ninety-one, had been all over the world, had interviewed highly acclaimed artists, and still looked forward to giving community lectures. If you asked her about conversation, she'd tell you, "Really talk about anything, if you are interested in it yourself. You will then project an enthusiastic voice and some aspect of life's varieties that may start a flow of conversation."

Mull that over, seniors. What are you interested in? What do you want to learn while you're sitting around with companions in your locality? What can you share that makes you an interesting companion, someone people are always attracted to? Try to discern why someone is appealing, why someone always has people clustered around him or her. The clues to sunshine are never out of sight or hearing. If I can offer one no-no, it is to avoid organ recitals. Nothing is more tiresome than listening to everyone's maladies.

There is a limit to some topics. One of the prettiest ladies in our residence was in tears one day. "I'd like to talk to you," she said. "I'm absolutely miserable. No one wants to sit with me, no one invites me to go to a movie, shop, anything. Has anyone said anything to you, given you some hint of why they are acting that way? Someone said I talk only about my grandchildren."

"Boring," I told her after a while. "What do the others talk about? What clues are you missing to gain favor with the group?" My suggestion was to ask them questions about how they had spent the day, what they made of the big problems (individually, of course) of the nation. Bring the attention back to them, learn a little about them, and remember the key word: humor. All it took was a change of direction. I have to admit her outlook changed very quickly, and she is socially happy.

We have all met women and men who watch what is going on between and among others and who are the first to broadcast any symptom of growing affections between people. First, recognize that they *observe*, the very meaning of which is from the *outside*. They are not to be trusted with your private dreams, which they will use to gain attention and favor with others, never truly entering into a meaningful friendship of their own. Be wary of the town gossip!

Respect your own privacy. You have the abilities, in retirement age, to contemplate more than one answer to a problem, to consider contradictory solutions to life's challenges, and to recognize how much in life is relative. These are the tools we need. We can begin to ask new questions, consider alternatives before jumping to new solutions, and make decisions based on a tighter integration of how we think and feel. This, says Dr. G. D. Cohen in *The Mature Mind*, is the underlying psychological engine driving the usually constructive (and emotionally challenging) midlife re-evaluation phase. We have greater respect for intuitive feelings. We are more flexible and more alert to the subtle ties of thought.

Practically every gerontologist will tell you that during these years, you will have more time to engage in developing satisfying relationships, discover new intellectual growth, and have more fun. Vibrant people have little patience for complainers. One well-liked person simply says, "Some people are still in the whining stage; they never grew up." Those who have a history of expanding their interests and achievements (not to be measured in dollars and cents) continue into later life with a positive view, searching for something they had never had time to do and opening creative new opportunities in life. After all, we are now told that the brain expands later in life, and we have the mental capacity for new activities. We are liberated. Worth reiterating is that wisdom is deep knowledge used for the highest good.

If there is anything to add, it is this: be alert to opportunities; remember that listening is an invaluable asset; try to establish confidence and trust ... and don't break that trust. You will find that your happiest moments occur when you abandon the sad things.

Let's pursue happiest moments. Hilda C. was one of three daughters. She always knew that her father longed for a son. When her firstborn was a boy, she was deliriously happy. The nurse told Hilda that she had sat all night watching and sharing such total happiness. Hilda added two more boys in quick succession. Triple happiness?

Mollie L. echoed such sentiments. After a series of miscarriages, she was scheduled for artificial insemination, rarely known or done sixty years ago. She was to have a long-awaited vacation with her husband; thus she scheduled the procedure for after her return. Like so many stories involving loosening tensions with long walks along sunny paths and evenings spent in bright moonlight, impregnation occurred. Despite a heightened risk of miscarriage and a premature birth, her son was born healthy and tenaciously clung to life. Today he is a successful physician in Florida.

Happy moments happen when you are engaged in pleasant activities. Men seek a sanctuary, a refuge, a retreat from the everydayness of retired living, a place for man time. Women are accustomed to clustering; that's as old as time. But men, in today's world, having been fully occupied in providing, welcome the societal change. They usually are primed for a more relaxed life, but they want to keep abreast of local, national, and world affairs, and they are open to new acquaintances,. They like to share their interests in politics, tales of their travels, criticisms of movies and plays, and so on. One of the arrangements the men at our residence make is a kaffee klatsch of their own. They meet in their special corner in the café, bringing printouts of current events and humor found in daily e-mail newsletters. They treat every topic with quips and tales of their own and have great mornings together. Who cares that the stock market *maven* takes himself seriously and wants you to do so also? Why not play Pundit yourself on the aggrandized postures of public figures? A grain of humor takes the bitterness away. Witnessing the congeniality as men of disparate origins exchange and analyze current and historical events makes you want to invite the president of the United States to come gain insight into senior-status democracy.

Here's one shared e-mail quote we can all see as a lesson in life. One day, a farmer's donkey fell into a well. The animal cried for hours as the farmer tried to figure out what to do. Finally he decided the animal was old and the well needed to be covered up anyway; it just wasn't worth it to retrieve the donkey. He invited all his neighbors to come over and help him. They all began to shovel dirt into the well. At first, the donkey realized what they were doing and cried horribly at the prospect of death. Then, to everyone's amazement, the donkey was silent. A few shovel loads later, the farmers looked down the well.

Every time a shovel of dirt hit the donkey's back, he shook it off and took a step up. As the neighbors continued to shovel dirt onto the animal, he would shake it off and take a step up. Pretty soon, the donkey stepped over the edge of the well and trotted off.

Isn't there some wisdom in every folk tale? Life is going to shovel dirt on you—all kinds of dirt. The trick is to shake it off and take a step up. Each of our troubles has a stepping stone. We can climb out of the deepest, dirtiest wells by going on with determination, thinking, never giving up. Shake it off, and take a step up! (Imagine that! A donkey can make an ass out of himself, or the ass can use his tuckus.)

Folk tales and long tales: it's all about insights into life and people. One evening talk turned futuristic and yielded some interesting ideas:

flying automobiles that upon landing could be folded up to fit on a stand until next needed.

One person answered, "I'd like one of those."

"I'll make it," said an engineer.

"I'll take it," said the other.

"It may take ten years."

"Uh-oh. Don't know if I have ten years. How about nine?"

Perhaps it is their relief from the working constraints of a lifetime, or just their comfort with themselves and their retirement status, but I find that retirees jest easily. They pick up a topic, and everyone is anxious to join the fun. Here's an example of what followed the above:

"How about wine pills of a thousand compressed grapes? You won't need a wine cellar. Easy storage and always retaining vintage."

"That's stretching it. You may get sixty glasses. Or eighty, maybe ninety."

"Now you're stretching it. Maybe forty, fifty, fifty-five … maybe even none."

This kind of teasing can be humorous and delightful but let me add a note of caution here. Teasing that makes the partner the butt of the laughter is not only tactless, it is distasteful. Even in an intimate moment. Pride and discretion are in the realm of caring. They are foremost in successful relationships.

Esther C. Gropper

**Dancing is a vertical expression
of a horizontal desire.
Bob—**

Health

Keep yourself in good condition. Couples owe that to each other. The widowed and the single owe it to themselves. You don't have to be in perfect health to enjoy a good life. Be prepared, if this is not one of your senior fears. I learned from my own experience that caretaking is the most enervating of all roles seniors are thrust into. Caretakers find themselves overwhelmed, overloaded and overstressed.

As someone knowledgeable in self-help, I coped. I suppressed my own feelings and activities to devote my time and patience to my Alzheimer's-afflicted husband. Somewhere in the fifth year, I found myself tormented, watching a brilliant Phi Beta Kappa professor of mathematics deteriorate to the level of a six-year-old. I found I had to interact with him on that level, as if I were the mother of this child, providing him with mental stimulus, alerting him to traffic on crossing streets, warning him not to wander when we were out together, averting his rude behavior with others, and assisting in a multitude of tasks that now seemed too difficult for him, including toilet and bedroom attention. One time, he called me from the bathroom, where I found him entangled in one leg of his shorts. In trying to untangle his legs, I was thrown to the floor.

I often wondered how much he understood of his diminishing facilities. Psychiatrists had no definitive answers to that question. I realized he sought my presence; that was assurance to him. He was agitated only when I was not in sight; consequently, I did not connect with senior centers for Alzheimer's patients. An option was to have a dependable aide, but she or he had to have presence for a while before I left for any personal relief time. Finally, my finger in the dam was not strong enough to staunch the stronger flow of deterioration. Bodily organs were affected from brain damage. At this point, hospice offered the most considerate and solicitous care.

I had to confront my own grief a second time in my life. I was losing my mate when I was eighty-eight, a vulnerable age when a mate is the very comfort to have. All the aging fears beset you. You feel that everyone is thinking, *how long does she expect to live? What can she expect of life at that age?*

But that is precisely when your resources, your strengths, your faith—everything mentioned thus far—is to be summoned to your side. Sadly, we face loss with the temptation toward self-pity and anger. Bereavement groups sponsored at your local religious center are helpful; therapy is offered by social centers, too. Seek the understanding and support of dedicated and trained professionals.

Poetry speaks to me often when my heart aches. I entrust the following excerpt from final thoughts by Frau Charlotte Schiller, wife of the poet who wrote "Ode to Joy," to which Beethoven wrote the music for the conclusion of the Ninth Symphony:

> Even if you had failings
> I should be forbearing;
> it is not love when one simply draws a beautiful picture in one's soul
> and endows it with every perfection,
> Rather this is love,
> to love people as we find them,
> and if they have weaknesses
> to accept them with heart-filled love.

Healing is a slow process winding through tunnels of darkness; every once in a while, a ray of light and promise breaks through, and eventually one will emerge to bright sunshine. Experience offers a more conciliatory view of illness and a healthier view of aging.

Let me share "Look to This Day," an uplifting and inspiring piece!

> Look to this day!
> For it is life, the very life of life.
> In its brief course
> lie all the verities and realities
> of existence:
> the bliss of growth,
> the glory of action
> the splendor of achievement,
> for yesterday is but a dream
> and tomorrow is only a vision.
> —Bob

"In its brief course/lie the verities and realities/ of existence" says a great deal about the closest relationship we have, that with our mates. When one of the pair takes seriously ill, the verities intensify. The main question to address is about loyal, consistent real love. Does illness cause a diminution of consideration, kindness, affection, loyalty, or sexual activity in your relationship? Is smirking, sarcasm, ignorance, sullen slavery, or silence in the air? Ah, beware the jabberwocky—the pretense of marriage!

Therapists have files of confided complaints, and I betray one of them when I tell you about a couple that wanted to save their marriage, but had the sort of scars that can take ages to heal—and sometimes never will. He had been having a long affair with his secretary, also married, but his conscience kept reminding him of infidelity to his wife and family, their struggles through the war years, his uphill battle to reach goals, and the intellectual stimulation he shared with his wife. That was a lot to weigh against furious sex. He confessed to her. Now she had her own battle scars, unexplained absences, a lack of affection, long silences. When he told her of his affair, her immediate hurt prompted her to think divorce. But twenty years of marriage is hard to disregard.

When he pleaded for another solution, she angrily asked, "Do you want me to give you permission to continue this charade? No. The only concession I'll make is for you to fire her and stop seeing her." He told her his feelings were "similar to a drug addiction." He'd need time. Despite the obvious provocation, she didn't let it get nasty. She wanted marriage counseling for both of them.

Inevitably, the husband's romance hit a snag. The woman would make any bargain to be with him, but that was jeopardy for him. He would not promise her any arrangement. Quietly she left his tent. He and his wife made their vows to each other, but he admitted that shortly after they were together, his wife's resentment of his philandering invaded their sexual activity. She asked him to refrain from arousal attempts; for her, they didn't work. Sexual advancesd stirred up the smothered anger in her.

But the rest of their relationship fared well. In fact, when he later became seriously ill, his wife's devotion erased lingering marks of infidelity. This often happens in later years for reconciled couples; they find deeper meaning in their alliance.

In a different vein, I came across one of those columns devoted to questions bewildering to the aging. This one, by Rabbi Gellman, appeared in the *Palm Beach Post*—evidently syndicated, so you may have read it also, but it's certainly worth rereading and heeding.

The question was about writing an ethical will, a spiritual or practical message to your family. "Take time," advises Rabbi Gellman, "to consider and recount the most important lessons you've learned in your life. Tell your children what you love about each of them and what you hope for them. It would also be a good idea to state your wishes regarding how you wish to be treated by doctors if you fall ill and can't express yourself. I'd also like to suggest you encourage family members to continue your charities and use part of their inheritance to help those in need. Send copies to all your children now, so there will be no misunderstandings."

I might add that the impetus to write this advice came from a questioner whose father died of Alzheimer's. The writer regretted that this advice was not given to her or her siblings until it was too late. My own son responded to this column by saying, "I'd like to hear it from you while you are still alive."

And a wife or husband might like to hear the sweetest of all words: love and appreciation.

Esther C. Gropper

> **Agreeable society is the first essential in constituting the happiness, and, of course, the value of our existence.**
> **—Thomas Jefferson**

There Is a Process for Choice and Change

The time has come to set aside childish things. It is time to be serious about play and exercise. –John Ratey, MD, associate clinical professor of psychology, Harvard Medical School

Living for Change

Build from what you learned in the past, of the past.

A great deal has been written favoring a positive attitude. I have nothing in my collective files savoring a negative attitude. Complaining and protesting are so much a part of human responses that I have often wondered why people don't think of better ways to be or get what they want. Wouldn't it be more enriching to use the same energy to plan what you want to be? Can you endeavor to make possible what you'd like to have? For starters, try a friendly chat with the person who bugs you.

When I and several other young mothers tried to comfort each other during WWII, spending an evening together with coffee and cards, one woman insisted upon our coming to her house every time, necessitating sitters for the rest of us. It appeared to be a selfish demand and, finally, exasperated with her, I asked her why she wasn't sharing our expense. She looked questioningly into my eyes, as if trusting me with what she had to say and expecting that it would not be believed. In a quivering voice, she told me that she was under care for phobias, and one of her most severe was being in unfamiliar spaces. I, who had grown up with a psychotic mother, understood immediately. I comforted her and assured her of our empathy. As an addendum, she and I became closest of friends. She became more like a sister than my own sisters.

Whenever I encounter moments such as this, I want to tell folks that it was not an easy lesson for me to learn for myself. In my book, *Not Far From The Tree,* I wrote about my early, tangled childhood: never living in one place long enough to make enduring friendships, always encased in darkened rooms with blinds drawn, windows sealed. I lived in an atmosphere charged with fear that a government agent would break down the door, seize my immigrant mother, and take her away, and I'd never see her again. Such were her paranoid terrors from a traumatized childhood. Adding to that dysfunctional atmosphere, the very air was charged with anger. Quarreling was habitual.

Was there nothing to lighten the atmosphere? There was a Steinway upright—oddly, my mother's pride and joy, polished daily to a high sheen. My sisters played well, my brother and younger sisters had unusually mellow voices, and at odd times, we actually had songfests that mother enjoyed. But my fearful mother would not allow us to invite friends. Nor did we three teenagers who wanted to be as social as other young people were invite someone in, never knowing what would ignite an outburst and never knowing when one sibling would destroy the peace of the other?

I remember suddenly waking up to orders to start packing; someone was hot on Mama's trail. In two hours, barrels and cartons were ready to go. We had no forwarding address to send to friends we might have started to know. Two hours later, we would be unpacked, our beds made for the night in another brief residence. My school records had three cards stapled together by the time I reached high school; most children had one card.

Were my siblings and I left with scars as a result? Yes. But the life source pounds against skin, and resolve erupts, seeking enablers for your dreams. Cinderella dreams are born from determination. The impetus for something better comes from many sources for all of us. The sadness around you can envelope you also. What's your choice?

From where do you find aid? For me, it was commendation from teachers. They encouraged me, directed me, and showed pleasure at my accomplishments. That was enough to make me walk miles to the library, rewarded with arms full of books for hours of quiet retreat. The belief that my good work was important to my teachers banked my keen desire to learn. I thought often about my own school experience when I became a teacher. I hope I passed the torch to other children.

I am a strong advocate of building from what you learned in the past. I sincerely feel you learn from what you like and from what you dislike. I believe living is all about choice and change. I believe the clues are all strewn about you. You have only to rely on your instincts for what is good for you or bad for you. I hope you have guides along the way to tell you when you're going the right way and when it is time to turn around and try another, better way. I believe that is the lesson you are born to learn, and you carry the lesson forth into maturity and into a fulfilled life.

When you begin to feel self-pity, remember Rudyard Kipling's poem, "If." Or consider this true tale: Dr. Frieda Alterman, ninety-six, was born blind but was determined to become an independent, self-reliant woman. She fulfilled her desire to become a clinical psychologist. Her husband, a neurologist/psychologist, encouraged her to pursue a profession, but she stalled, choosing to be a homemaker and bringing up her two boys in a traditional way. Unfortunately, her husband whom she described as "gorgeous", died quite young and she was not prepared to be the wage earner. Crazy thoughts ripped through her mind: *I'll rob a bank or pilfer groceries.* She found that "need breaks iron." That was when she followed his advice and took business courses to attain a B.A. in commercial education. In 1932, the tides turned for her; she made a lot of money in real estate. She had this to say: "Everybody has his worth. Find your own worth. You must know your own self-worth. Be determined, fearless, push everything (not everybody) to the hilt. People are nice; they help you. You can't sit and wait for someone to fix things for you."

Esther C. Gropper

If you found your own worth, don't be too hard on the negatively patterned people—those who anticipate the bad and the worst or catastrophic. Allow space for people with moodiness, melancholy, suspicion, who show wariness of new surroundings and strangers. They can't help it, according to Dr. Goleman. They are reacting to their right frontal brain activity, as contrasted with left frontal activity in generally social and cheerful people, who enjoy their time intermingling and engaged in its sphere. They enjoy good moods, are self-confident, and rarely are depressed.

Esther C. Gropper

**Love and Doubt have never been on speaking terms,
Exaggeration is a truth that has lost its temper**

—**Khalil Gibran**

What a Time We Live In: Changing Mores

We are reinventing ourselves scientifically. Ask any senior or wounded veteran about replacement of body parts (teeth, knees, arms, legs, livers, and so on), and they're apt to chuckle at their own answer. Why not repair our personal lives as well? We would gladly submit to chemically altered neurological brain receptors now being tested and testing well—to improve important biological functions. Further advances are being made in memory and cognition, regulated genes, and personalized drugs for individual bodies. Are we willing to face the ethical questions raised in these speculations? The visions are beyond belief.

But let's think of something pertinent: longevity. Assume you've been given this gift, or modern medicine has procured it for you. How will you use it? What would you want to still accomplish, attain or choose to do? In my role of conscience reminder, what's stopping you now? Doctors will tell you that you already are living an extended life, but biotechnology still has more to offer. Will we become a new specie as a result of further modifying biotechnology and gene changes? How will the changes affect relationships, communications, goals, and so on? Is it worth exploring? What will be the reverberations of longevity? Are you seeking long life?

Then you will have to set up a regimen and discipline yourself to follow it assiduously. And yours may become the example for generations to follow.

What we have available now are random suggestions such as a somewhat recent recommendation to drink red wine. You'd have to drink seven hundred bottles for it to have any effect. Or is being drunk the actual goal? Why?

As we live longer, relationships with children, grandchildren, and great-grandchildren become very significant. We consider it a blessing to share their life experiences, attend events, and gain a glimpse into their futures. We might play a part in decisions. Life offered me an unusual opportunity to bond strongly with my granddaughters. These young college women were at crisis moments, turning points in career and romance. For various reasons, their parents were not accessible for what they classified as unconditional consultations. They reached out to Grandma, who was doing e-mail at its inception. Grandma had been writing articles about connections and bonding with family through technology. They knew Grandma could be trusted with confidences. The consequences of their exchanges of e-mails resulted in a book *Not Far From the Tree*, in which Grandma shared her experiences as a child, as a maturing adolescent, and as an adult. She had been part of the struggle for women's rights. She recognized parallel dilemmas and crises in the lives and careers of her granddaughters. She had questions for them about social and cultural relations confronting career women of the current era. The questions Grandma asked still need resolution. Let me share the following pertinent excerpts from my book, *Not far From the Tree:*

> I have questions about satisfactions women will find in their equal status. Slap up against their gains in the marketplace, they have natural inclinations toward mating and reproducing. In essence, women want a normal home life and compelling careers.
>
> Here's what dilemmas your generation has to resolve: Different lifestyles from those of the past. My kids have an aunt who is a successful doctor; her husband is the homemaker. Another aunt matches status and income with their uncle that redounds in being equal. Arrangements bring males into greater sharing of family and home chores. Do they make concession

to each other? Of course! They are living the changes of our times. You and other women like you, who have advanced degrees and ambitions, want a crack at the highest CEO in the country. How will your drive affect you? Normal females who attract males: You have normal sex drives, normal desires for stability of home and children. Are your children going to be future byproducts of day-care centers and nannies? Can those lives be enriched, as yours was, nurtured by concerned mothers who were there for crises or after-school activities? What breed of people will emerge from children brought up by nannies, many of foreign birth and culture? How much stress in business and home will they be able to absorb? We already have about a 60 percent divorce rate resulting in derailed family life.

My generation had its super moms juggling family, home, husband, job, and social life—five balls up in the air at once. The cyber moms of your generation are adding more balls. You've added separations because of travel needs, competition of careers, unwillingness to subordinate drives to the partner's success—not the least of them will be deciding on a central location of operation—complications of home life conflicting with complications in corporate life. How far can you stretch your limits? How mush flexibility do you have? You know I support your ambitions. I just wonder whether you will have to surrender other aspects of life.

As I fast forward to the present, I see responses to my questions in articles from men and women of this generation. The Week in Review of the *New York Times* features Sunday Opinion columns that talk frankly of tensions between couples. One I particularly noted was in the January 24, 2010, edition, titled "My So-Called Wife" by Sandra Tsing Loh, which opens with these remarks: I am stricken with the peculiar curse of being a twenty-first century woman who makes more than the man she's living with—first with a husband for 13 years and now with a new partner—the proportion of American marriages in which the wife makes more money rose to 22 percent in 2007 from 4 percent in 1970.

She then romanticizes (or so it seems to me) about the idealized married life of a former age when a wife's duties ended with the pipe, slipper and Manhattan cocktail lovingly laid out. She is the caring, listening wife of his dreams. She then flips to the other side of her that fantasizes herself as the husband of that wife: In the end, we all want a wife. But the home has become increasingly invaded by the ethos of work, work, work, with twin sets of external clocks imposed on a household's natural rhythms. And in the transformation of men and women into domestic co-laborers, the art of the Wife is fast disappearing. So in the meantime, I may need to settle for a man who can simply make a decent tray of Manhattans and, while you're at it, pussycat, make mine a double."

Even in this capsulated version, don't you detect cynicism in the way each role turns out? Is there a solution to either equation? I discern acceptance, and in acceptance, isn't there compromise? And is compromise satisfactory? Lasting?

Is it any more agreeable when the wife is the co-provider on a lesser level? If hers is lesser, is the man expecting more of her share of the living or chore arrangements?

While I fire an array of questions, you're probably formulating your own pertinent questions. In all of these, solutions have to be found, or marriage as a whole flounders, cracks, and crumbles, and we are left with sand waiting to be washed to the sea. And mores will shift as well. New views and methods, as mentioned, are experiments. Children out of wedlock are no longer scandalous (Sarah Palin's conservative cohorts haven't dared to deplore or denounce her daughter's out-of-wedlock child). This is no slight impact. The social structure of our society continues to change. What will evolve? The jury is still out.

Let's have a look at an example of dual roles in Jodi Kantor's article,"The First Marriage," printed in the New York Times on November 9, 2009. "The union of Barack and Michelle Obama "is an ongoing negotiation between two strong-minded individuals over how to balance work and family, ambition and principle and the demands of privacy and the public stage.

"Barack and Michelle Obama have never really stopped struggling over how to combine politics and marriage: how to navigate the long absences, lack of privacy, ossified gender roles, and generally stultifying rules that result when public opinion comes to bear on private relationships.

"Along the way, they revised some of the standards for how a politician and spouse are supposed to behave. They have spoken more frankly about marriage than most intact couples usually do. The bumps happen to everybody all the time, and they are continuous ... even as an attempt to vault over the forces that fray political marriages (could politics be any more demanding as an occupation?). People who face too many demands—two careers, two children—often scale back somehow. The Obamas scaled up.

"In their early days of marriage, Michelle had her job as a corporate lawyer while he was in Springfield developing his political career. Living separately this way was tantamount to that of being a single mother. Barack helped as much as possible: on top of juggling jobs, he paid household bills and did the grocery shopping—when business was done for the day, he always drove home that same night."

Worth sharing are comments each of them made pertaining to their rough moments. One of these was the cost to her career when he seriously entered politics. He said, "I think that it was important for us to work this through." Both of them agreed that each had their ups and downs in their marriage. Perhaps their experiences can help young couples realize that good marriages take work ... and can work. Perhaps Michelle Obama will write the penultimate guide for career, marriage, children, and social-minded couples that want to stay coupled.

My own granddaughters are trying to code their versions of the twenty-first-century marriage. One is a physician, one a physical therapist, one a corporation official; all have children, and all are wrapped up in their multiple roles, determined to enjoy home and family as well as careers. Joelle, my granddaughter, enjoys her full time position with a high tech firm. She takes an active role in their education and other activities. How does she do it? You might want to visit her blog. Site: www.practical parent.com. Joelle became a mommy blogger after being asked by multiple people for her insights into education, discipline and work-life balance as a full time mother of three. The practical-parent style is a blend of personal anecdotes with published research to help reader-parents make informed choices. Again, these are works in progress. The jury is still out but will hopefully present a good verdict for the future life of families.

Esther C. Gropper

**To exist is to change,
to change is to mature,
to mature is to go on creating oneself endlessly.**

—Henri Bergson

To Exist Is to Change

The beaches are littered with shells of what seems like an infinite variety of conchs, clams, and crustaceans that had shed their shells to adopt more mature forms. Snails abandon their shells, snakes shed their skins, and so we continue up the evolutionary chain, seeing human embryonic changes as adaptation continued. Nature is replete with odd adaptations, such as the auk that is seagoing half the year and airborne the other half. How do the amphibians change and adapt? Imprinting signals their motions. Flocks, schools, and herds among all species are not only a show of grouping, they are methods of species protection, imprinting, and survival. Necessity was the motivation. Humans follow many of these instincts for securing their territorial boundaries. Ingenuity led to weapons, and this distinguishes the "higher" form that adapted to shore, mountain, and plain living. As maturing and aging segregated the stages, each individual sought his independent abode, changing from tribal to independent modes. In much of the world, population growth and work centers are so crowded that high-risers are the answer. Isn't this comparable to bees weaving hives bigger and bigger? Beehives and high-rises!

Humans experiment with different lifestyles, not unlike ants and animals. Longer life now challenges the imagination. Human beings, in the Western nations, have outlived traditional modes of living. They are in flux, at this point of time, to find the most comfortable and most satisfying way of living. How will they change?

On the plus side, I think we learn to have more patience, not only with others but ourselves. We have only to look at ourselves: Bluma in a wheelchair, I just recently abandoning the walker. What about your level of patience? Have you experienced a tremendous expansion of patience? Let that patience fuel your focus and determination. We spoke of assets taken from the past; chalk those two up on the board for me.

When I became a widow, I found myself alone in familiar places where I had been two, doing things that had been done as a twosome. It was like losing the other half of myself. It had wandered off to another place without asking me to go along. Why did life go awry? Didn't I have more living to do with him? And what about that space he left behind, especially where I turned in bed and the cold part of the sheet touched me instead of his warm, nestling groin? I'm sure many other seniors experienced such complexities after the death of a spouse, or other nutty things they found themselves doing to keep sadness at bay. One of my closest friends filled her days going to department stores, purchasing gowns and shoes that would have suited her earlier lifestyle, and then returned them the next day. She had one short runway hour before her mirror, shed tears, and went on another spree the next day. She did that until she really confronted herself in the mirror, asked herself what she could do with her life, and became a successful antique dealer. She drew on her passion for art objects, antiquities in clothing, and accessories.

But back to my story: eventually, I was introduced to Barney, with whom I shared many interests. A problem developed when he proposed marriage. He was retired and spent half the year in a Florida retirement community. I loved teaching and was at the zenith of my career doing innovative curriculum planning. I visited him at his winter Florida retirement community. I was completely out of my element in retirement developments: age and activities.

I did marry Barney. Between us, we planned living up north with winters in Florida. As I've mentioned before, I was in a new marriage, a new environment, with a new opportunity before me. I had just to awaken the determination that had also been part of that life and put it toward writing. Oh, I did have to learn new techniques to apply to a market out there—quite a different endeavor from academic writing. I had a chance to write children's stories for my grandchildren or stories about my family. I learned to objectify some of those stories by converting to fiction techniques. By the way, that was fun and a learning process. I joined writing classes and groups. With readings, exposure, and critique, my own style sharpened. What a thrill it was to receive acceptance with a check! I also got rejections, of course, but many editors take the time to offer suggestions for changes that make stories ready for commercial acceptance if they detect a good story or technique. New writers have to be ready for disappointments.

Writers have to be prepared for people who ache to show their tales. It doesn't take much of a brain to understand that acceptance or praise is what the person is looking for. I recently had a visitor here who was introduced to me as a writer. She immediately asked me if I would read her collection of family stories. They were warm, pleasant re-creations of experiences with her mother, her children. Delightful pieces! Were they publishable? I didn't have to get into that, but I could say they were wonderful to share with progeny and as a legacy for family treasures, especially if pictures were added. That is reward unto itself.

Yes, added Bluma, pictures illustrative of their lives, along with anecdotes, would prove to be treasures. Women have home stories to share, particularly at this time in their lives, when they have time to pursue such projects. They love their handiwork, because they are used to keeping their hands busy. One group at our residence is knitting shawls for patients in the Care Center.

"Can you imagine," remarked one lady in a group knitting scarves for our military, "we're back to fingerless gloves that free fingers for triggers or scarves and caps 65 years after the ones we made for World War II? Reminded of her incapacity, Bluma said "My hands won't do that for me." She was referring to her arthritic hands but you could see her active mind at work, thinking up topics for discussions that engage people in other meaningful activities.

In constant pain from arthritic hands and severe back disc

deterioration that confines her to a wheelchair, and suffering from poor eyesight, Bluma concentrated on this project with me as well as lectures. That personal comment about her incapacity at this stage popped out, but she quickly was back on track and talking about artistic people around us. She referred to a bridge game with five players, the extra player sitting out a round. Hazel sat out; she began sewing a pillow she was making. She is one of those women who never has idle hands. Bluma will always pick up on positive actions that enhance life—always showing compassion for others, always offering a smile and cheerful conversation. Somewhere, fate doles out predictions for our golden years. We have to blindside the handicaps, albeit temporarily, and find sunshine.

"And the men, too. I will have more to offer in that respect, but what about you, Esther?"

I've already told you how I faced major crises twenty-five years ago, but the recent past is flooded with deep depression over Barney's severe mental loss and behavior that you'd expect from a six-year-old. I was doing everything I could for his comfort, but it drained me of interest in life. I did consult an analyst who emphasized all the things I knew to do and was doing: taking an hour or two off to attend a class or give a class, taking Barney with me for his own diversion, or attending a yoga session, but I needed a renewal of energy and commitment. Of course, I could and did continue lecturing, giving book reports, and planning programs with our senior learning staff. Still, the unanswered hollowness haunted me. It wasn't until I seriously sat down to write. In this phase of my life, my mind and activities felt synchronized. I was completely in my own world, and liking it, I feel that artists, musicians, and anyone absorbed by the arts has this experience This is the third book I've written in my later years.

Incidentally, men like to share their expertise and interests. They do. Informed men lead discussions about investments and politics. Women also are involved, eager to learn and participate in lively talk about current topics. Seniors have to search out learning centers that offer classes to stimulate their minds. Many older men and women have plenty of expertise to offer society: scientists, geologists, meteorologists, physicians, and so on. Philip Leto, JD, a sem-retired attorney, recently started Sterling University. He is a traveling lecturer with a phenomenal storehouse of judicial, historical, and literary information in his brain. He unfolds and analyses critical periods in the history of the United States, impounding effects from relationships with other countries—their politics, their cultures, interweaving affairs—and how they impact on international events. A tireless speaker, he keeps audiences riveted for an hour plus. With a fund of knowledge at his beckoning, he answers questions with specific facts and impinging stories. Life does not have to be dull. * (You can email sterlingu@tampabay.rr.com for more data.)

I do not intend to ignore those who are suffering. We mentioned compassion and patience. One does need both, especially when an acquaintance prolongs talk about pains and losses. Well, the listener does have to offer some way to divert interest. Change the slant of the subject. Show your awareness of tremendous advances in health research, or offer healthful hints on food and trim figures. The moment you divert to a topic that is provocative or engaging, conversation becomes lively; you've found another avenue to explore, whether it's a topic in the news or a magazine or just a personal anecdote. During such conversation, your own life expands. (Example: the tremendous advances in space exploration and the questions it opens in the mind.) Our wheelchair residents are devoted to the programs already mentioned, but there is no shortage of wellness topics, therapies, and physical activities to alleviate pain and anxieties. You have only to reach out to the residences and agencies that provide then.

We thought we had offered many ways in which aging people can enjoy comfort and pleasure but one resident alerted us to another possibility. "What about pets? My wife, who adores her little schnauzer, is ready to walk anyone's dog, to assist anyone who is ill or handicapped. I have a friend in another community who walks three or four dogs daily for a small fee. The pets give and receive tremendous affection, so necessary to lonely people."

We have a small group who go to the zoos and animal shelters to assist the staff. Some go to the public gardens to help there. The truth is, there are endless opportunities dto enrich later years or assist others to do so.

Esther C. Gropper

Ah Love! Could thou and I with fate conspire
To grasp this sorry scheme of things entire
Would we not burn it in a pyre
Remold it nearer to our heart's desire?

Based on a Persian, Farsi poem by Hakim Omar Kayyam

Accepting the Changes

Deep down we know we have to change some actions that imprison us, and yet our ingrained values and habits put up stop signs. *How can I ignore a family need? They've always depended upon me.* Or, other emotional demands get under our skin: *How can I go off to another part of the world where I have job offers and do what may be a change of career for me? Why do I become a slave to others' wishes and not mine?*

I am asking hypothetical questions but turning the focus on you. You likely have your own questions framed on your memory wall: the job you didn't take because the impact on your children was questionable, the house you didn't buy because everyone cautioned you about the mortgage market. Just a page back, I said you have the capacity to change what's out of order. Thus, it is a matter of choice. What is your choice? Are you making the right or the good choice? I refer you the book **Emotional Intelligence**, in which you may find new concepts that lead to better insight and judgment.

One thing our generation has to admit is that we were brought up in a different social system. There was obedience to restrictive family mores. In contrast, our children had more freedom and independence in making decisions. We had to work hard and make sacrifices for advancement. Our children had the possibility of higher education, many without loans. We clung to familial expectations. Our children were given foundations of our trust in them and offered more freedom to make choices. The changes are many between generations, and we continue to witness the societal specter of evolution. We can afford to give ourselves space for changes that will serve us, with one caveat: we do not have the right to insist upon change for others. Nor can we change some things at our convenience. Changes that affect more than yourself require consultation and agreement. We may have to offer what is feasible and functional. Balancing needs and wants against reason and emotion is important. When the unexpected, such as illness, occurs, the caretaker should not have to buckle under the strain. Opt for alternatives that give both sides consideration. Consideration is a long string that sews hearts and hands together. Consideration is knotted on both ends.

What happens when fate separates us from our mates? This is probably the weightiest change we can experience. Some couples are wise enough and caring enough to discuss the consequences to be faced. Too many of the widowed are confused because the partner handled the funds, leaving the other confounded by household expenses and mutual investments. Financial conditions should be clear for transition. Enough has been published regarding the importance of caution and preparation in this area.

My thrust here is to accept the new stage of life, to plan and program for years of a comfortable, contented, and gracious life. The perspective for the coupled or single older generation recommends internalizing that *now, now* is when to seek answers to questions. *Now* is when your ideas ought to be thought out and shared with others of similar age group. *Now* is when you should start with confidence, to know what you want for the rest of your life, and that should include tackling potential difficulties. If you are married, you should express your wishes, as should your spouse; if single, target your investigations among informed people. Serious questions should not be left to chance.

My husband once told me that if he ever developed Alzheimer's, I had his permission to have him institutionalized. Yet, when that time arose, I could not do so for emotional reasons. I told him he might consider that a breach of promise, but I would prefer him home among familiar surroundings with an aide, so I could have time for myself.

He looked at me with tearful eyes and kissed my hands. My decision went against professional advice, but I had to be faithful to my own conscience and/or emotions.. The other way is more sensible. There will be more to say about this problem in the next chapter.

For our purposes, let's look at the male elderly. Are men's interests different from women's? It will not come as a surprise that men seek a refuge for themselves. Men, as do women, seek a sanctuary; they refuse invitations, retreating from the everydayness and sameness that can make later years of retired living atrophying. Inwardly, they may be seeking stabilizing activities, an order to their lives that business or professions formerly provided habitually. They like a place for man time and man talk, with coffee at their arms' reach. This is not intended to derogate or complain about the women in their lives; that is a different topic.

As I paused to greet them one morning, their subject was food. One man asked another what he had for breakfast.

"A bagel with smoked salmon."

"Sounds good!"

"Not for the salmon."

They are often heard in laughter. A great way to start the day.

I've heard men comment on the difference in maternity clothes today from those their wives and mothers wore to disguise or hide the growing embryo. Women today portray posture. The rounded bellies are displayed with pride, as if each were going to give birth to the second messiah.

One grandfatherly man said, "I'm especially disturbed by the young kids, high-school age, who flaunt their pregnancies. Theirs seems a mark of status among their peers. They've done it!"

"My guess," responded another, "is that they set off mixed emotions among the other students. I'd like to think girls particularly have been reared to behave morally and to consider premarital sex and pregnancy shameful. Certainly, facing child rearing as a husband and wife gives the child a respectable link to society."

My granddaughter tells me that in her school girl talk about the courage it takes to ignore public disapproval and scorn, to mock church and family in pursuit of their own glorification of sex, and to flaunt their bellies in defiance of parents, teachers, and priests. How stupid can teachers be? What difference does it make what I see in Bruegel's painting *The Wedding Dance?* She wants us to see the pleasures of simple peasants. If she looked closer, she'd see pregnant ladies whooping it up with peacocks. Grandpa, the girl was right on. You have only to look at the exposed men to get the point.

Grandpa couldn't resist the temptation. "Did you mean that pun?" Better to drop it there, but the discussion didn't end there. Another man insisted upon being heard.

"What this does is make adolescents inquisitive. They vie for the privilege of feeling the infant move. They want to know every detail about pregnancy. Who knows how many others are enticed by the process? After all, Hollywood stars are having children out of wedlock, and rock stars have their antisocietal, rasping voices blasting the airwaves. It's trendy! It's all Peter Pan in modern undress."

The kaffee klatsch talk ended with Robert's bon mot: moralists are people who scratch where others itch.

The next morning, the men were at their table, ready to tackle another dilemma of the day. And, surprise! It turned out to be about romancing and marrying again in their senior years. Very few wanted to marry, because the *now* held prospects of caretaking, of foreseeing a custodial role twenty-four hours a day. Perhaps they had not found the first marriage blissful. They would like companions and mates with whom they could share adventures, yet they refrain from commitments that add to their responsibilities. Several had been living alone, and they liked it.

And so, we come to a consideration of what it means to live alone. You breathe deeply and feel independent. No more domination, acquiescence, or compromise. But independence for the elderly is a toddler learning to be surefooted. There may not be a secure hand

Dance until the Music Stops

an arm's length away. The nearest supporting wall resembles a Gaudy structure. And so, one step at a time, balancing yourself with freedom and adventure, you find a desirable way of life for yourself.

Then, something really surprising happens: an attractive/handsome face across a crowded room (a senior center, a residence) awakens a memory of romance like a cue card. There just might be a desirable person to get to know, a person with whom to start a conversation that may run into and through cocktail and dinnertime. And, what the heck, it's more appealing and more desirable than a good night's sleep. It is not only likely; it happens often. And when it does happen, it evokes an extraordinary and intense feeling.

Now a new set of questions arises: how can you make these late years comfortable, agreeable, and enjoyable? Let's have a serious talk! What are the options, and which one is better for you? You discuss the traditional way. Are you open to new experiences?

Another surprise: seniors are testing and adopting new living modes, emulating the younger generations. They're sharing homes, sharing expenses, sharing chores, and sharing conversation and good times—a balanced life. I have met the achievers and the strugglers. Given the choice, the wise one would recommend becoming an, achiever! (Any dispute?)

Sid came to our residence eight months after his wife died. All the pins under him collapsed. He didn't want to see friends, eat with others, or join any activities. His daughter felt he needed to be in a place that offered opportunities to be with other people and a setting where sociability prevailed. She finally convinced him to sell his big house and take an apartment that was manageable. A former neighbor who now resided at the same residence persuaded Sid to play bridge with him. That was the afternoon he looked across the room and saw the woman he'd like to know.

She had the bluest eyes and warm smile that cut the veil over his eyes and heart. On subsequent evenings, he found her consoling and restorative. She introduced him to opera and found he had a rich baritone voice most enjoyable to listen to. New interests for him in theater, concerts, and lectures began to fill the hollows in his heart. They were affectionate toward each other, and it came as no surprise to hear him say he loved her. He would say daily that his feelings were sincere and profound, that he could not bear the hours when she was engaged in other matters. She felt the intensity of his love, his kindness, and his concerns for her. Perhaps it was partially their ages and the threatening limited span of life left for people in their late eighties.

Vera and Chuck met at a senior dance and found more than good dance partners. A month later, they took a cruise together. (That's a good test: proximity when the only way out is overboard.) Back on terra firma, their feelings were rocking rhythmically. They are sharing an apartment. Marriage? Been there already, having experienced its encumbering legalities.

Marge and Sam shed running pants for pajama pants and were living together for two years when Sam took ill and needed surgery. Marge could not visit because she was neither wife nor blood relative. When he recovered, they married. They would not encounter that block again! Affectionately attached to Sam, Marge did not question the potentiality of recurrence or unexpected problems, and Sam progressively was stricken with serious illness. Did Marge make a poor decision?

But Marge had genuinely fond feelings for Sam. Abandon him? Not in her nature. That brings up the question of options. But first, shouldn't we consider the risks of marriage in this context: the endurance that illness demands and the sacrifices to be made, particularly by the caretaker? We can set the scenario and project ourselves into each of the probable scenes. What role do you see for yourself? It's best to be honest about your feelings; these are serious questions. Everybody lives with the unknown, is knocked around by the unknown, and learns the power of the unknown. Consequently, nobody can claim to know it for you.

As a counselor and as a subject in my own confrontation with a husband suffering from Alzheimer's, I could not abandon him. We had twenty-six years of marriage and friendship, commitment, and interdependence. By the end of the six years, until his death, I held myself in noble esteem. No one could criticize my concern and care. Every consultant from different agencies I called upon advised care centers or around-the-clock aides. We could afford aides (an essential factor), but I was there when the only one he wanted was me. As long as he could see me, he was compliant. He could trust me to be there for him. We made him as comfortable as possible until he died. And I? I was exhausted, emotionally and physically. I needed help myself to recover from that experience. Do I recommend faithfulness under trial? Are you stronger than I? I do recommend time for ourselves. Sacrificing ourselves makes us martyrs. Do you want or need that?

What options are available? Strange shifts have occurred in lifestyles. After long introspection, do they find living alone the best option? Do you have enough self-reliance? If there's a shadow of a doubt and you need the comfort of others around you, consider the social environment of a senior residence and/or the nearness of relatives and friends. You have the possibility of two or three more decades of living than those of the past. Assure yourself of the best option for yourself or yourselves. You want and can have good dwelling. In a stage of life that can offer rich rewards, make a home where sincerity abides.

Esther C. Gropper

**Living is like quilting
Piecing together visions of the future:
tentative, promising, budding, fulfilled,
ultimately a spread of the story of your life.
e.c.g.**

Sunshine and Rain in the Ebbing Years

Amnesia. Dementia. Alzheimer's. In each of these mental states, the spoken words are forgotten, repeated, forgotten, and repeated again and again until this perseverance sets nerve endings on edge. I had heard this complaint about living with an Alzheimer's victim many times, but I didn't know how trying it could be until I faced the symptoms in my own husband.

Apparently, the strongest personality traits become more pronounced with the diminution of mental faculties. My husband's innate sense of humor, the quality that endeared him to me, dispelled the sadness and despair of the future. Even as we were aware of his diminishing mental acuity, I could enjoy his company. His wittiness remained.

On a recent rainy summer evening, we emerged from a concert hall to the thunderous clapping of thunder. The fortunate ones who had thought to bring an umbrella pressed forward. The hesitant looked heavenward for signs of abatement. The exit was crowded. My husband began to fumble with the folded umbrella he carried with him as a talisman against bad weather or against capricious spirits he imagined hover around him.

"Stand at my side." My husband's voice had a note of anxiety. He was fumbling with the latch on his folded umbrella.

"I can't do that," I responded. "People have to pass. I'll stand behind you." He continued to grapple with the mechanism; his hands were trembling. I tried not to show impatience.

Finally, the umbrella snapped open, and he handed it to me, saying, "Listen, you have to protect your coiffure. I'll walk behind you, but make sure to cover my head, or I'll be accused of being wet behind the ears."

Before claiming our car at the nearby garage, we stepped into a coffee shop. We both hoped the rain stops before we took the parkway home. He was enjoying his muffin and coffee. I saw crumbs clinging to his lips and chin, and I motioned to him to brush them off. Using his fingers, he failed to find the right spot.

"Use your napkin," I suggested.

"Well, that wouldn't take much marksmanship, would it?"

His blade-edged humor was alive in him, but mostly he shuffled and slumbered. He would ask the same question at intervals during the day and get the same answers, apparently forgetting he had asked the question already. He was struggling against locked gates in his mind; beyond were swampy regions that were strange to him.

When did he who had volumes of history stored in his brain, he who could trace at a instant's cue the progression of languages following conquests, give substance and quotes from the Bible or great philosophers, start raising his eyebrow, his teak-brown eyes showing bewilderment? But then, unexpectedly, the flashes of jocularity came forth.

He began to talk about Diogenes Allen, a theologian we had heard lecturing that week, the name sparking recollection of the Greek philosopher with so great a reputation for wisdom that Alexander the Great was prompted to pay his respects to Diogenes. The conqueror stood at the portals of the Pantheon, so impressed with what he heard from the learned man that he asked how he could bestow some favor on the humble man. "If you would, sir, stand a bit to the side. You are in the path of the sunlight."

My husband's manner was calm, quiet, which was why he liked where we lived, on a quiet street, in an old Victorian house, with rocking chairs on the porch. Despite the view and the comfort, he would choose to stay indoors and read his newspaper under lamplight. When I suggested he go outdoors and sit on the porch, he answered, "No, because when I get up, the neighbors will say 'He's off his rocker.'"

When did he begin to show reluctance to see people, dine out? In a sense, I was living alone again. The companionship that had sparked and invited a second marriage was gone. The philosophical, clever conversation was over. The one thing that could have induced me to trade independence for interdependence had set a trap for me to be caretaker again. I sustained myself with his occasional humorous responses, with the fun he made of serious subjects. I had to settle for quips.

Our friends were often impressed by his hearty appetite and disregard for calories in his selections. "Don't you worry about calories and weight?"

"I've been consistently slim over the years. I weigh in at 145 pounds for my yearly exams."

"Never any more?"

"Well, it depends upon how many coins I have in my pockets."

Recently, solicited on the phone by a local funeral director and asked about burial arrangements, he answered, quite honestly, that his family had a mausoleum in his native state and didn't need their plan. But solicitors are persistent, and this one had another service to offer and entice the listener into a contract. "We can make arrangements to fly the body to that state."

"Well, yes," he was quick to respond. "We might have a deal if you will accept my Delta SkyMiles."

I relished these moments. He was showing the one quality that distinguished him from other men. He had the ability to make me laugh and dispense the sadness that change was bringing. I actually envied his ability to make a quick retort that closes an argument. At a recent community meeting, where a fractious board member vowed to vote against a candidate for the board with the words, "Over my dead body," he answered, "Where do you want us to send your body?"

He endeared himself to me this way, so when he said, "Stand in front of me," I did shelter him, reaching out to hold his hand. We walked together in the rain.

Esther C. Gropper

> Writing and talking about one's life is
> a way of making sense of one's life.
> —E. C. G.

> I'd better mince my words a little better;
> it'll be a lot easier to eat them later.
> —Bob

Memoirs

A wonderful way of sharing your life with family and friends is writing short memoirs. Short passages are good to start with, and if you find yourself writing longer pieces, consider that an encouraging advancement of the genre. It worked very well for me when I found that remarrying took me away and family, friends, and career, all of which left me feeling homesick and blue. The change coincided with my sixtieth birthday, an age referred to by many as going downhill.

On the road downhill, I met poets and writers. I found a new career as a recognized writer. I met Etta Ress, who started the movement for senior learning centers, later to be the model for others countrywide. I spent thirty years giving classes and promoting new ideas for classes, presiding for three years. I didn't have a lonesome moment after that.

Etta Ress, a retired supervisor of media in the New York City school system, soon found other eager minds to share knowledge and current topics, which led to the organization of senior classes. Enthused, she conferred with President Eissey at Palm Beach Community College. He saw merit in her plans and convinced the governor to provide space and funds to start programs. The program became a model for many colleges across the nation.

Reuniting in the sunny south with many people migrating from up north presented another whirlwind of activities. With our renewed friendship, Edythe Marlowe and I discovered many similar interests that we began pursuing together: travel, opera, theater, ballet, books, and good food. That included cooking good food. After we had shared years of sending gifts—birthday greeting watercolor miniatures from her in exchange for poems from me—we compiled a cookbook, *Close Friends*, as a commemoration of a beautiful, long-lasting friendship. I wouldn't call this a downhill life. In fact, these past three decades, despite many unhappy events, have been most gratifying, most loving, most fulfilling. Retirement—a refirement essential—can have all those components.

If you're having trouble writing, a simple device does the trick: just get it down! Every family has a mighty tale to tell. My family has a history of sharing diary accounts they believe are meaningful to the rest of the family. Consequently, we have bonded by stories. We have been able to span distances—from the Atlantic to the Pacific. We never feel more apart than a e-click away. Let me share an excerpt from *The Journey: The Experience of Becoming an Ironwoman,* by Tracey Downing, that anyone would want to share and preserve.

IRONMAN or later on included IRONWOMAN is a triathlon including grueling events in the world of sports. It is also one of the most inspiring. Ironman triathlon features a 2.4-mile swim, 112-mile bike trail, and 26.2-mile marathon run, all in succession. Entrants have 17 hours to complete the event (from 7 a.m. start to midnight. This race was held in Canada, August 2003.)

I clutch Tom's hand as "O Canada" is sung to us over the PA system. The cannon sounds and we kiss good-bye. I will not cry! We slowly take to the water. It's so shallow that we walk a long way. Tom holding me back so that the faster swimmers can go out before us so we don't get clobbered as they pass us later. And then we're swimming. The lake is glassy; the water is clear; suddenly I'm calm. I'm swimming. I've been doing this since before I could walk. "Ouch!" I exclaim into the depths of the lake as the first of many fists to hit me during that 2.4 miles makes contact with the top of my head. Elbow to my side. Heels in the stomach. I must be getting close to the first turn because the crowd around me is definitely converging. I can smell the smoke on that side of the lake. I make the turn and get pushed around some more. *Pick on someone your own size*, I'm thinking as some bigger guys swim by me. Headed into the next tturn... Ah, there's something underwater. Yep. I forever have this nagging paranoia that lurking somewhere in open water there is something waiting to get me, and there it is—I close my eyes as tight as I can. I remember hearing something about scuba divers during one description of the course I open my eyes a little, like watching a horror movie, and see two divers sitting on the bottom waving up at us and giving us the peace sign. *Phew*, I think with a little giggle. After one more lap of elbows, feet, and arms grazing different parts of my body (unintentionally, of course), I finish the second loop and head for the finish line. I sight on the two balloons marking the finish line and finally, after an hour of being pummeled, I have open water. There's no one around. I was so relieved to finally be able to get into a rhythm that it didn't even occur to wonder why I was suddenly alone. I just kept sighting on those two balloons. The starting line is coming into view. I'm minutes away from being finished with the first event of the day. I can hear the announcer. I can hear the spectators and then I hear, "You! You're going the wrong way." I feel a tap on my shoulder. I stand up and look around a little dazed and confused, realizing that everyone else who was finishing the swim was at the other side of the beach. Bummer! I put my head down and swim to the actual finish. I emerged from the water amid screaming spectators and friends. What a joy to hear my name yelled by friends as they recognized me coming out of the water. Across the timing mat and over to the wetsuit strippers. I lie down on my back. Two people tug on my wetsuit, and it's off in a matter of seconds, off to get my bag and then the change tent. I sit down and take a deep breath. A volunteer is standing next to me, dumping out the contents of my bag, handing me everything I need, helping me get dressed ... I head out of the tent and around to my bike.

Esther C. Gropper

There are continuing descriptions of the next two races and then the concluding lines: I finish feeling great with a big smile on my face and turn to hear my friend Tim shouting "There she is! If ever there was a look of an Ironwoman, you've got it. Congratulations T-dog!" After 14 hours, I was truly entering the finishing chute. I saw Thom's family screaming like crazy people—never knew those Alaskans could be so rowdy. I slowed down to let the cheers sink in. Arms overhead, plumping fists, ear-to-ear grin, as I let the cheers sink in. The bullhorn sounding, maybe not as obnoxious this time, with Jason announcing "Tracey Downing from Los Altos, California, you are an Ironman!"

N.B. *The Journey:* Becoming *an Iron Woman* is a memoir written by Tracey Downing.

> Memory: The struggle of man against power is
> the struggle of memory against forgetting.
>
> —M. Kundera

Memoirs are the voices of memories: Keep in mind that Wisdom is accumulated knowledge.

Memory is the handmaiden of wisdom. We are all fearful of signs of Alzheimer's. I have seen the afflicted develop all kinds of defenses or alternative actions while there is still a thread of self-identity. But even barring a stroke or Alzheimer's, a certain amount of memory loss is evident as we age.

Take heart! Our memory resists the total crash of the computer. In fact, our brains have no known storage limits, sometimes amazing us with the surfacing of scenes of long ago. Unstrung, the brain has infinite space in which memories reside. I am often reminded of a passage in the play *Equus* in which the psychologist remarks on the fact that despite the vast experiences one has had, the brain holds fast to particular images or events that mold our behavior. Why, for instance, will one remark by your father, of the many he made in his lifetime (or any equivalent remark by someone), unalterably affect your growth? Why would a smell, a sound, the feel of taffeta trigger remembrance of something long past? Why, out of billions of dendrites, millions and millions of constellations of brain cells, do particular memories surface? Dr. Golden states that we only remember what stands out—what is unusual, personally significant, or unpredicted—or what we intentionally memorize. Does something of our pervasive memory affect our choices of friends, mates and associates?

At a reunion of friends who hadn't seen each other for sixty years, they shared memories, pictures, and stories about children and grandchildren. When they spoke about memories, they laughed over incidents, gossip, and plans.

"I have memorabilia but lack current recall," said Elaine whom we know as Tommy, the youngest at seventy-nine, "so I devised a means of recall. I tell my husband to remind me of the package I stored in the pantry ... but no sooner do I say that than I've already forgotten what I stored."

Memory is the chief vixen for seniors. Because the problem is so common and uncomfortable to think about, we shed discomfort with jest or a laugh. The more serious dementias should warrant medical attention. But to get back to the reunion, the attendees talked about living in senior communities, of going to concerts, the opera, the theater, and their favorite dining spots. Most important to them was the old friendship in their hearts.

They could speak freely and trustingly of their children whom all knew. The kids had shared schools, religious milestones, beaches, and boats, so much a part of their family lives. What makes such friendships special and remarkable is living history and personal growth, especially when the children are on their own. Marvin remembers the revealing bikinis and beautiful, sexy bodies.

"Do you still wear bikinis?" he asked Pearl, who still was tall and slim.

Always quick-witted, she answered, "Yes, but now they call it underwear."

In this digital age, when e-mail and text messages are the modes of contact, this group retained the direct art of conversation, with all the facial expressions and gestures that enhance their tales. They had to pause occasionally to take in air. Young people rarely have long, delightful discourse; they're too busy checking messages and responding in silent words. They work in lines of cubicles bound in by glass partitions. It is after work that they head for gyms to stimulate their bodies or join the living world at a bar. You can't blame the rush of noise that emanates from there. They seek the free air of earlier years. They depend upon buzzing centers because many eventually turn homeward to the television sets that are again silencers, until it is time to change the pace ... and face retirement. Well, this is the time to plan for the change. Plan one that won't disappoint you.

Esther C. Gropper

I can't resist an empty page
to test my talents as a "stage"—
at least as member of the club
who count their birthdays from
seventies up!
Up's the word, my cheery friend!
Up's the gesture in the end
that gives a final touch of grace—
the ace in the hole of
advancing age!

e.c.g.

Are Your Juices Still Flowing?

A colleague of mine was trying to console me when my husband died.
"You are fifty,"
"So?"
"You have half of your life left." (She was practically on target.) "Let me give you a page out of my experience. I, too, was in my fifties when I was widowed. One morning, I faced myself in the mirror. I told that woman looking back at me, 'You've grieved. You may grieve a lifetime, but you have a lifetime left to live. Start today! What am I going to do to make Pauline happy today?'" She did that, and what a whirl she had: visiting exotic places, enjoying good times and good lovers.

The breadth of her vision might be intimidating but surely you can consider small joys that are easy to implement. Take a moment to weigh the distractions that prevent you from enjoying the day. Put them in the mind's column of "Things That Can Wait." - that can wait while you heed the call of your soul. Find something to make you happy. Once addressed, the seed is planted. Let it grow!

In other ways, face questions about your life; face crossroads; face potential alternatives. By the same approach, I faced the writing of this book. Was I ignoring difficulties? Where would I get time and energy for research? No. On the contrary, the motivation was steady as I began to think creatively. I felt as if I was accomplishing something. My immersion in studies and my interviews became profiles of life. My introspection spurred new insights. The process itself was exhilarating and absorbing. During a writing session, I felt I was being myself. Any form of activity you've wanted to try? Okay, you're past basketball or climbing walls. But there's still dance, yoga, choral groups, and a host of arts and sports to absorb you.

The juices will start flowing, and you'll discover new dimensions to yourself.

Let me remind you: Cheerful people live longer.

A reporter for a Florida newspaper, wrote something that if it were true would be sad. He received thousands of letters from people laden with private anxieties and passions, but not from people over seventy. Excerpted from his comments: perhaps their shaky hands couldn't pen the letters. The contents from midlife readers contained questions about aging symptoms or marital problems. Older people presumably had resolved, reconciled with, or simply accepted their marital problems. Maybe they've declared a truce.

That's one opinion, but my guess is that golden oldies still care enough for each other to air differences and summon learned ways to avoid ruffling feathers. I know one couple who addresses angry words or moods with a schooled approach: "You're evidently angry or upset about something. Am I the cause? Can we talk about this? If you're just going to spill angry words instead of neutral words about causes or reasons, I'll never know why. We should sit facing each other at the table." (The table should be clear, with no dishes around to throw!)

This approach sounds more cheerful than Daniel's correspondents!

And if we are talking about advanced age, you're not inclined to travel anymore. You have ties to children, grandchildren, and for some lucky ones, great-grandchildren. Your trips will be to see them, not the Leaning Tower of Pisa. But what real reason do you have for not trying a low-stress cruise or Elderhostel, now called Road Scholar.

Check the actions and reactions in your bridge game. Will alternating partners work better? Need a change from sports programs? Westerns? TV soaps or shopping stations? Has something begun to grate on your nerves? You and your partner have different viewing tastes? How about another comfortable TV nook in the apartment? Then get together for that late-evening snack! Just a reminder to keep romance glowing!

What contributes to romance among the elderly is vast experience and a lexicon of romantic words and gestures, a practiced knowledge of what pleases, doing such actions with ease with personal attention and magnetism: that's charisma! In a room full of people, a man's eyes are fixed on a woman's on the other side of the room. Yes, it's a familiar line of a wonderful song, "Some Enchanted Evening," and he knows and she knows that they will linger a while with each other. Thus begins what is incredibly perplexing to the younger generation, not less to themselves. A deep relationship is forthcoming, and the pair is on their way to becoming a trusting, affectionate, caring *item*, as senior parlance goes.

Another surprise evolves with the testing of lifestyles familiar to younger sets: the questioning, sorting, selecting, and arranging of their lives together. Move into one of their apartments or homes? Give up both and select one that is suitable to their joint needs or wishes? Go it alone, with each having his or her own place, but with sleepover dates? This may sound much like the ways younger folks are patterning their lives, but they did break the rules. They certainly risk more than older folks, putting aside any scoffing their grandparents receive. So? Who's afraid of the big bad wolf called gossip? He can't hurt you. You have a strong companion: love.

And, surprise! Very few women want to marry, for the same reason very few men want to marry: the risks of marriage in advanced age. Like many men, they have been living alone, and they like it.

Others say they aren't ready for drastic changes or are embarrassed before their families. And not surprisingly, they don't want to relinquish an independent style of living. "I don't want to have to account for what I do or take on responsibilities again," they say, or "I don't want to become a caregiver. That's a risk I don't want to take again," or, "I won't give up my freedom to make choices—to compromise my choices. I achieved freedom the hard way."

In these cases, like many of the younger set, these couples have overnights and/or weekends together. The neighbors might talk. So what? Show your maturity and humor. Let them get their kicks that way. You, on the other hand, have a partner, a companion, a lover—whatever your choice brings.

A satisfactory choice, as AARP research has found, leads to better health for the partners, less stress, and more free time to increase their satisfaction with their sex life. With emphasis and research on expanding lifestyles telling us we don't have insurmountable obstacles, options are yours to explore. Who says there aren't good years? Medicine already offers some help for our aging ailments, and seniors can continue to enjoy intimacy long into their extended years. It's not inevitable that sex should stop when people get older.

I chuckle at the story one of our residents told of seniors visiting a different neighborhood and hanging the "do not disturb" sign. Seniors do RVs frequently. They're doing the traveling they always longed to do. Now, unencumbered, they are finding adventures in motor camps and seeing the country with new perspectives. So with that in mind, the next time you see an older couple in a camper with a bumper sticker that says, "If this RV's a-rockin, don't you come a knockin'," cheer them on. Sex can be meaningful at any age.

Esther C. Gropper

**A man's real possession is his memory.
In nothing else is he rich.
In nothing else is he so poor.
Alexander Smith, Dreamthorp**

An Addendum

Stored In Memory

I am a strong advocate of building from what you have learned in the past. I sincerely feel you learn from what you like as well as from what you dislike. As a child, I liked what I saw and did in my friend Alma's house. I spent many a Saturday morning at her home, making butterscotch and peanut-butter sandwiches for lunch. We played board games, of which she had many. I loved the praise and encouragement from her parents and the love that pervaded the home. My memories of those playdates with Alma are overlaid with what I learned from that friendship. One in particular had a number of lessons for me.

One Saturday, she asked if I'd like to see her father's library of medical books. She led me to a playroom where the books were impressively shelved. She took down a heavy book on anatomy and opened it to pages that showed illustrations of female and male genitals. We were rapt in our study and did not hear her father enter the room. He had quickly noted what we were looking at.

"Would you like me to explain anything to you?" He followed that with the question, "Esther, how old are you?"

"I'm eleven. Today is my birthday. I am eleven."

"If today is your birthday, aren't you having a birthday party?"

"We don't have parties in my house."

"Hmm. In that case, you should at least have a birthday present." With that, he reached into his pocket and drew out a half-dollar coin. My eyes felt as if they'd pop. "You can buy whatever you like to celebrate a big birthday like eleven."

Whatever I liked? My child's heart ached for a painting set I had seen in the window of the candy store on the way to school. Surely a half-dollar in 1930 was a fortune and could buy that paint box. After profuse hugs and thanks, my swift little legs took me to the cloudy, slimy-windowed store; the colors on the paint box glowed like halos in my dreams.

I timidly entered and asked the price of the paint box. The storekeeper answered that it wasn't for sale; it was a prize that came with the punchboard he had on the counter.

"Each punch is one cent."

"I'll try it."

My first try had a white center. A pink center meant a prize.

"I'll try another" ... and another. Eleven cents had been spent from my half-dollar, and I was getting sick from the gooey crèmes. "You said there were ten winners in every fifty chances. I don't think that's true."

"Little girl, why don't you go home?"

"What if I gave you my fifty-cent coin and claimed the ten prizes? I'll take the whole card. I don't even want the candies, just the prizes ... or only the paint box." I was feeling anger, but I was willing to make a deal. Even as I look back at this incident, I can't believe I was brave enough to say that.

"I am not selling you any more. You go home."

An eleven-year-old can be intimidated by a rough voice and mean face. I learned something that held for a lifetime: If it's too good to be true, believe it. It's not true.

I learned what I wanted in my life, in the future I would make for myself. I believe living is all about imagining and planning. I believe the clues are strewn all about you. Growing up is about exposure to possibilities, choosing and relying on your instincts for what is good or harmful for you, and knowing when to turn around and try another, better way. You meet influential people along the way. Knowing people who can explain and expand on what may be right or appropriate for you

Dance until the Music Stops

is beneficial. Advice and guidance should be acceptable. Giving thought and making decisions to the paths open to you is your obligation, not that of others. I believe that is the lesson you are born to learn. You carry cumulative experiences into maturity and toward a fulfilled life. You are the sum total of what you made of all you experienced. And then there's the old expression: the house you live in always has room for improvement.

And in "your house," what is important to you? How do you look at your accomplishments? How do you feel about your relationships? Do you have attributes you haven't inventoried?

Esther C. Gropper

Live all you can; it's a mistake not to.

—**Henry James,** *The Ambassadors.*

Imp of the Perverse

The imp of the perverse gives no warning. He/she is a stealthy destroyer. Here I was, jauntily saying, "Yours is the responsibility of making your later years lively, enjoyable, and free from care," when he summoned his forces to strike me down. You can't trust the golden years—they're only gold plated! Fool's gold! The glint is from the sun; it is tarnished under the clouds! Isn't that what the cynic in us declares?

It happens! I was planning a trip, a jaunt, an excursion, an adventure, plotting all I would do in the next year, when I suffered a blow- a stroke. It was almost a knockout blow. My eyes went askew. I was standing and walking as if inebriated, disoriented.

What about the plans I had had, the places I still wanted to see? I wanted to redeem my adventure, share events with my progeny. I needed that surge of determination that had always prompted me to bounce back, but the bounce was slack. Hands reached out to me, and I heard encouraging voices from surrounding friends and family, from a therapist or two. My ears heard the rhythm of life; my eyes, which had been thrust awry by the stroke, were becoming less fuzzy and shadowy, perusing travel brochures again; my gait was overcoming imbalance. More particularly, as a boxer who has a bad round, slightly battered and bruised, springs up at the clang of the bell and gets back in the ring, determined to beat his opponent, so I was resolved and ready to continue control of my life. Best of all, I was able to return to this manuscript with more insight and commiseration for those who had lost agility and their ability to handle their needs of the day.

Esther C. Gropper

    Incidentally, a romance that had started before that crisis now deepened. I attribute this to the sympathy and support of the man I had met. We had begun to share mutuality of interest. We felt inclined again to dance, to spar with words until we laughed at each other's wit. We saw in one another a sparkle of affection, both of us more aware of the tenuous aspect of life and health. We began to treasure the time we could spend together. This was my third deep experience with love, and when I think of the affection—the closeness of that relationship at an age when I did not think it possible to share life so deeply—I realize that a great part of the loneliness that aging people feel is that blanket of love, that protective, reassuring caring that gives reality to you—the person you are, your individuality. And there is someone sensitive to your feelings, which sparks your own warm concerns for the other, and it overwhelms you. Let me share a short poem that is imbued with the feeling I speak of:

> *LOVE*
> is a burden
> that two hearts
> when equally
> they bear
> their parts
> with pleasure
> carry.
> But no one alas!
> Can bear it alone.

(Submitted by a friend who wishes it to remain anonymous.)

    I think back to the day I met my first companion here who was a relative newcomer to our residence. I was in the bridge room, engaged in a particularly challenging contract, and I looked up to catch my partner's approving nod. Instead my eyes met those of a man at the table across from ours. He had a friendly smile on his face. An upward lifted eyebrow seemed to ask, "Who are you?" From where I sat, he looked familiar.

I have to explain that last remark. I had been active in the senior program of the local college for close to thirty years; I had served as a lecturer/instructor there and later done programming for the eager elders, eventually presiding over that division. All in all, hundreds of seniors took my classes in memoir writing, book analyses, play reading, and so on. I relished the intellectual exchanges among thinking people, people who remained dedicated to learning even as they were aging. I frequently met and exchanged social moments with them in theaters, concerts, and markets. I thought Sidney was one of them.

We exchanged glances. He seemed so like one of the senior college members, who had been friendly, interested in keeping the mind alive, and a master of the art of luring a woman to him. (That proved far from the truth.) Catching sight of him was a strange experience, more of the *some enchanted moment* that a man and woman capture, at first glance across a crowded room, wanting to know each other, to engrave their impressions, as an artist would, of the configuration of eyes, nose, cheeks, and erectness of head and shoulders—to catch symbols of attitudes, letting that widening smile erase lines of age, the imagination stroking the paintbrush with a rush of color to his face. I blushed as well, in a rush of feeling, a curiosity as I speculated on what it would be like to know this man.

I was startled when he called across the room, clear enough for all to hear, "Can we have dinner together tonight?" The room seemed to be fired with strobe lights. I felt as if everyone saw the pictures in my mind, recognizing at once the romantic spark in my imagination. Passion lounges in senescent bodies, still there to be stirred awake.

Perhaps this is a place to pause to ask the question, "What makes some women more attractive than others?" (We'll follow with aspects of men.) This is not to deflect from the pride all should take in appearing neatly groomed; it's always a welcome trait. But the emphasis is on *more*. One man said about a popular woman, "She has a glow." Perhaps everyone could name one attribute that makes a woman attractive, but what such attributes will still be with her when she is seventy, eighty, or even ninety? Beauty? Stature? Poise? Charm? How about charisma? You may want to compare meanings with friends, but for me, it's a force that is patently there: magnetism! Star power! Yet, these stars share the stage and lighting. And if they lure the other sex, it should not come as a surprise. It might raise eyebrows to suggest figuratively that some don't want paparazzi around them. They want quiet lives, loyal companions, and good conversation, especially as they grow older.

Mull that over, seniors. What attracts you in a potential mate? Some people are always attractive. Why? The clues are never out of sight or hearing.

Esther C. Gropper

The tinsel words of love should be suspect
Because they don't give the same excitement
as those seriously conveyed.
Some people have a hunger for gossip and use it
as a substitute for
warmth and belonging
—John O'Donohue

Awaken the Brain

From hunters and gatherers, we have become cybersharers. The occupation keeps some people at the keyboard nine hours a day, often in repetitive tasks. If you're not a Tweeter or a blogger, you're behind the times. But take note, younger folks as well as older ones: a sedentary life leads to low energy levels. Awaken the brain! Brain volume increases with exercise; exercise optimizes learning and improves the ability to focus, decreasing anxiety and depression. There is the choice. If you want to keep young, keep challenging yourself with physical and mental exercise.

An added benefit will be stimulated curiosity, all because neurotransmitters like to keep sparking, and exercise is the way to keep them at their tasks. Can there be a connection here between optimal mental health and degeneration ... dementia? A number of neurological studies are researching this possibility regarding the onset and progression of Parkinson's disease.

Walking, insists my massage therapist, is the key to expanded brainpower. Why blame your genes for keeping you from doing? You are the governing force. Give your genes a chance to work for you. Join a walking, hiking, or biking group that gets you outdoors and peps up the body. Frank takes groups out to bird sanctuaries where nature displays her palette of colors and her assembly line of landscapes that protect the secrets of bird and plant life. Add "learning" to the list of attributes you gain when using and moving the inner circuits of your body to optimum, with the bonus of breathing clear air in the great outdoors.

What interferes with the path to success is fixation at some point; failure to see the caution signs or to resolve a hurt. I am reminded of my stepdaughter Judy from my second marriage.

When I met Judy, she was already a grown woman. She had a master's degree and planned to continue for her PhD in Persian literature. It sounded as if she were on the right path; I thought so.

My own daughter, a practicing optometrist, had been married to a young lawyer for two years. They were a good family with good values. Among those values, for both, was career success. Many factors disturbed their happiness—not least of which, in my estimation, was very little time to live a honeymoon period. As time went on, resentments festered, and my daughter confided that she wanted to divorce Bob. She called me frequently to air her emotions. We had long conversations that could occur any time of day and night. I had learned to listen.

On one of these occasions, Judy was sitting at the table with me, she drinking her fourth or fifth cup of tea in the late afternoon. She was privy to our conversation. It lasted about forty minutes.

After I hung up, Judy asked, "Does Laurel know how lucky she is?" Startled by her question, I remained silent for a moment as she went on. "I could never talk to my mother so confidentially. She never showed me she cared about what was doing. In fact, whatever I did was wrong in her eyes. And my father? When he came home, he picked up the newspaper and made right for his study until it was time for dinner. And at dinner, they never focused on me but beamed at the stories of my brother's accomplishments. I was the bad seed."

I was shaken by her picture of her childhood. I had had nothing but favorable opinions of her mother and father—how accomplished they were, how good their marriage seemed. No one can measure which child in the family gets the worst deal or how it compares with children in other families. But Judy's sadness was a *tableau vivant* of a child not favored. It was close enough to my own feelings about being unwanted. I had stored that sorrow in a closed corner of my heart and then eased it out, pinprick by pinprick, over the years until I could just think about it as a stumblebum that I had little place for in my life.

"Judy," I asked, "how old are you now?"

"Forty."

"You've carried that baggage around long enough. What do you want of life? What do you want to be? What do you hunger to do? That's what should be your concern now. Shed the baggage. It's like a bombshell threatening to destroy everything for you. Dump it!"

I don't know if it had any effect on her. She remained a restless individual with queer habits and found her haven in Turkey when she went there to study the language and culture. She taught English to students there, remaining there as long as her visa lasted. Now she continues to spend half the year there, half in the United States. Perhaps her associations are more dependable there. Perhaps they are, because she is very generous to the people she knows there.

I know my solutions to my problems differ from hers. I changed my life many times. I feel I've grown into a much different person from when I started. I know that I have confidence in myself, and that quality is precious to me. I have one great trait that derived from neglect, but not completely: I don't encourage sympathy. I'd rather have respect for what I am now.

I am reminded of an experience that may better convey what I want to say. At the time of my first appointment in the New York City school system, I was sent to a school at the very tip of Brooklyn, an area originally inhabited by Jewish families but later home to Puerto Ricans. The children were from poor families, often coming in without breakfast. In bad weather, we rubbed their rain-soaked or icy toes warm and gave them food to fill their tummies. Parents didn't mean to neglect; they were just impoverished—in many ways. They were deprived culturally as well as financially.

I was asked to sit in with the social worker while she talked to the father of one of these families. During the entire discussion, the man was turned away from us. After he left, I said I hadn't expected that behavior. We were trying to help him.

"You misunderstand," my coworker said. "You wouldn't know that this is a terrible embarrassment for him. To be the least bit critical offends his Hispanic machismo." She then added, "You were born with a silver spoon in your mouth."

By that time in my life, I had learned not to let my mouth hang and my eyes blaze. I had gone through many changes—changes through acculturation, changes in life. Could she know how many times my father swallowed his pride to ask for a neighbor's compassion for his mentally ill wife? Could she know that I had schooled myself against my dark childhood memories of pain and anguish, that I had tucked those memories away in a well-guarded tomb? In truth, you can rewrite your life and create a new scenario instead of re-creating the acts of the past.

Dance until the Music Stops

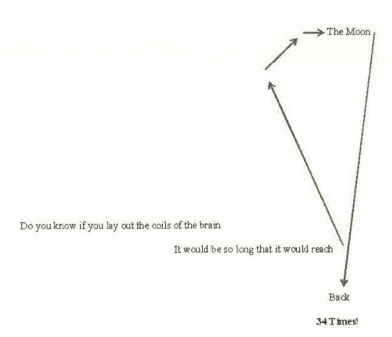

N.B. The diagramming is my way of connecting the course of thought.

Esther C. Gropper

**Crisis is an opportunity
to use a coil of the brain.**

—D. O. Cohen

You're Primed for Adventure

As G. D. Cohen noted in *The Mature Mind,* much of aging research conducted during the twentieth century emphasized improving the health of the aging body. As a result of this research, life expectancy and overall health did in fact improve dramatically. Aging research at the beginning of the twenty-first century, in contrast, expanded with the strong focus on improving the health of the aging mind. One fact is that the brain is more flexible and adaptable than once thought ... not only is it more flexible, capable, and adaptable than once thought, but it also retains its capacity to form new memories, which entails making new connections between brain cells. It can grow entirely new brain cells—a stunning finding filled with potential. Older brains operate in a dramatically different way than younger brains. Older brains can use both sides of the brain for tasks, whereas younger people use only one side to accomplish.

Engaging in brain and mind activities is like going to the gym for body exercise, but in this case, it's mental potential that is expanded.

In another section, Dr. Cohen recommends seeking out a community education center, joining a book club, participating in a current-events discussion group, attending writing workshops, or doing something else that challenges you. Consider volunteering.

Sunny S. has volunteered for worthwhile agencies. She offered suggestions. Keep adding to your list of things to do: dancing, board games such as Scrabble, crossword puzzles, Sudoku, playing a musical instrument, reading, knitting, gardening, traveling, developing computer literacy, learning a new language, reading plays. It is amazing how many sign up for play readings, trying something new, challenging themselves to sound like Cary Grant or Tallulah Bankhead. If you attempt a genealogical study, you uncover lost relatives. These pursuits make you a more interesting person, leading to a promising sense of life and control. And to surprise you, they boost the immune system and positive emotional responses. They also add to your network of friends.

Social engagements are associated with better mental health and lower death rates. The clock in us doesn't go backward to childhood but offers an opportunity to make our longer years worth the aches and pains. We don't deny having those nasty arrows pricking nerves and weakening muscles, but if we stretch and move, keeping the body in motion, we can diminish the cramps and aches. These strategies have an impact on debilitating illnesses. This is what gerontologists advise. Disregard them and you'll miss the more rewarding aspects of aging and view the process as dismal and depressing.

Want more encouraging facts? Activity reduces blood pressure, reduces harmful stress and brain damage, and combats loneliness.

Well, it turns out that you can teach an old dog new tricks. I could have told them that. In my teaching and administrative planning programs at the Lifetime Learning Institute (Palm Beach Community College) I found seniors who were excited by the desire to learn, to exchange ideas with others of their generation; they actually soaked up every new development in the arts and sciences. They were more eager learners than the undergraduates with whom they shared tutorials; they were the questioners, the prompters, the researchers. They surprised the undergraduates; they inspired them. Judgment is better in the aging person. Your mind has been maturing through rough waves and ebb tides. Your psyche has stored the experience of responding to past problems and challenges. You're apt to retain the good decisions, why you made them, and how you engaged the efficient faculties for later trails. There's no moratorium in the aging stages of challenges. What you may find is that you're able to face problems with a calm disposition.

You may become the wise grandparent who cuddles a little one and helps wipe away the tears.

This scene makes me recall the story of the little boy whose puppy died. No one could console him. Grandma tried by saying, "My darling, it should comfort you that your puppy is up in heaven, and God is taking care of him."

The little boy's eyes opened wide. He looked at his grandmother and replied, "What would God want with a dead puppy?"

This approach may not have assuaged his sorrow, but his ability to latch on to logical reasoning did get him on to another track.

Now, here is a surprise for you. As you get older, you begin to use the other hemisphere of your brain. If you were left-sided (language, mathematics, and so on), you will begin to have stronger visual recognition, skills, and artistic development. Both sides are now used. That's a very encouraging message. The brain functions are being measured intensely now in many research centers around the world.

Not only does research find that as we age, we lose negative emotions such as fear, anger, and hatred, but research also indicates that in place of these negative emotions, we gain judgment, skills, a willingness to explore, and a desire to watch new ideas emerge and develop. That seems to account for interesting elderly people we meet who are active in areas they never tried before: the salesman who had an ongoing interest in history is now giving talks about current events that show their relatedness to issues embraced in the past, historically worthy or unworthy, or the retired teacher with reams of facts with connections to politics and effects upon the people.

When I retired, I wrote about the experience of *refirement* (not retirement, a downbeat word)—not the least of which was getting socially connected. You will find people with similar tastes and persuasions. You will share good hours that way and fulfill one of the major needs of human beings: companionship! There's an old truism: water seeks its own level! You can believe it. It even follows for dating systems.

Good dating systems mean to establish trust in their service. They

Esther C. Gropper

know that the subject is sensitive, that intimacy and communication are tender issues. Somewhat like a science, meeting the right person is the essence of love matching. Finding a mate is tantamount to lifelong fulfillment and happiness. It has to be a serious search, and dating services know this. The better ones help you with your search. One company has a lengthy questionnaire covering 29 dimensions of personality: curiosity, intellect, emotions (anger, mood, and conflict issues), family values, education, spirituality and traits (humor, sociability, ambitions, goals, and so on). For a match to happen, compatibility had to be demonstrated between two people in 25 areas. Rival services offered differing approaches, such as avoiding the creep factor or criminal factor. This is a big business. No recent data is available, but if in 2003, consumers spent 300 million dollars on dating services here in the United States, think of what it is now with evidence of satisfaction. Senior Dating Systems are available and making contacts are more comfortable than at a bar. If you seek companionship, try it but know what you want in a mate. Be honest with yourself. Go for it.

Esther C. Gropper

Let there be space in your togetherness and let the winds of the heavens dance between you. Love one another but make not a bond of love; let it rather be a moving sea between the shores of your souls.
—Khalil Gibran

Sexuality in the Elderly

When I was a bride, I was told to approach love and cooking with reckless abandon. Now, my friends gibe, should we be sexless and eat takeout with abandon? Do you go along with that?

From the time Masters and Johnson daringly asked, "Can that one facet of our lives, affecting more people in more ways than any other physiological response other than those necessary to our existence, be allowed to continue without benefit of objective, scientific analysis?" In 1966, very little significant and plausible information has been provided regarding the sexuality of the aging. This phenomenon of living beyond the four-score legend, which opens the manuscript to a vibrant, healthy, active life enjoyed by people beyond seventy, eighty, and ninety, can be meaningful and enjoyable. And surprisingly, many are still married or coupled in modes unheard of a few generations ago. Why do many younger people believe that one's sex life ends at sixty when there's a flood of TV ads on Cialis and Viagra? Doesn't that imply continuing sexual desires?

Comforting to them is to know that not everyone has daily visits to doctors, and when older people do have appointments with doctors, such visits are not always dismal, but encouraging about the future. It's not always easy to discern the age of a woman today. Youth enhancement and age-supportive medications are part of a major industry that researches and advertises their products. Would that science would concentrate on the organ-debilitating problems of aging or disseminate information on how to keep mind and body healthy and alert!

Esther C. Gropper

Recently, I went for consultation with a cardiologist. When the nurse presented my credentials, he came out to greet me.

"I think there's an error here," he said. "I am looking for a ninety-year-old woman." When I answered that I was that woman, he addressed the waiting people with disbelief. "You have to share your secrets." Well, I am. I am offering any number of suggestions in this book on making life distinctive and good, all based on living proof that aging is a normal process with fringe benefits. And to repeat: Cheerful people live longer!.

The psychoanalytic theory of Sigmund Freud (1905–1962) still remains one of the few comprehensive theories, but it does not focus on the specific aspects of sexuality in older persons. (Eddy N. Elmer, Simon Fraser University.) Geriatrics was not a popular study in medical school. Neither was gynecology. Half a century before the advent of antibiotics, Dr. William Stewart Halsted, a diligent forerunner of modern surgery, established a successful therapy for a noxious sexual disease with a successful irrigation of the urethra. He was the first successful surgeon of radical breast-cancer removal. He propounded cleanliness, sterilization, and major European practices, one of which was surgical gloves, to reduce infections and deaths after surgery. Dr. Halsted, one of the leaders in forming plans and staffing for the Johns Hopkins Hospital, recognized the need for a professor to head a gynecology department. He lured Dr. Henry Atwood Kelly, who quickly became one of the Big Four of Johns Hopkins who advanced surgical procedures and aseptic techniques that gave women courage and hope with their afflictions.[4]

We are beginning to be more comfortable with discussions about the intimate organs and functions of our body. Scientists, doctors, and pharmaceutical laboratories are relying on good writers to convey advances and theories guiding experimentation. An article (in a release by About.com) discussed sexuality but did not give a precise definition of orgasm other than in objective terms i.e., physiological experiences in the body, including heat, muscle tension and release, heart rate, blood

---

4   For more information, see *Genius on the Edge* by Gerald Imber, MD.

Dance until the Music Stops

pressure, and so on. No mention was made of a star-studded sky or what the French call *la petit mort*, the best translation of which is "It's to die for—not from!" One can find better allusions and better details in fiction. One statement I found in applying theories to sexuality in the elderly, in which stratifications of age appears, refers to historical influences on values and attitudes toward sexuality, which themselves have a direct impact on the interactions occurring in older individuals' sexual relationships.

Sexuality in the elderly can be defined in a number of ways. Foremost, sex can be considered more than merely a biological act of procreation or pleasure. It is a complex social interaction between two or more people. It is the dynamic interaction involving each partner's own personal values, attitudes, disposition, cognitions, wants, desires, and behaviors. Furthermore, sexual behaviors, including acts of courtship, foreplay, and coitus, can be interpreted not simply as means to ends, but as acts imbued with meanings that are interpreted differently by different people. Together, social interactions relating to sexual acts and the meaning attached to these sexual acts can change over the life course and may change significantly during older age.

Meanings and interactions can be seen as changing in a number of ways, and as able to significantly influence the negotiations that occur between sexual partners, especially depending on the degree of correspondence that occurs between two attitudes, desires, behaviors, and so forth. For example, a lack of correspondence might cause disagreements as to when, where, and how often sex will occur. Not only could this lead to sexual dissatisfaction, but it could also strain an entire relationship. Such discordance would be an important factor to consider, especially in light of Kaplan's observations, made in 1979, that interactional difficulties may be just as troubling for a sexual relationships as such simpler factors like erectile or organic difficulties caused by physical conditions.[5]

The meaning attached to sexual behaviors could be seen as one of

---

5   E. G. Cooper, 1988; Sakheim et al., 1987; Schover and Jensen, 1988.

the most pronounced factors that differ between sexual partners. As individuals age, sex might no longer be seen as a reproductive act, but might come to be appreciated as an act of affection, intimacy, pleasure, or leisure. It might also be considered an act that reaffirms one's continued physical functioning or virility. If partners come to differ in the meanings they interpret in these various aspects of sexuality, then the timing, amount, and quality of sex might change, leaving one or more of the partners dissatisfied or unfulfilled.

Older people can experience some negative changes in sexuality. For example, memory loss (of pleasure) may upset the balance of a relationship and surely dementia can destroy the paths of concentration. Various drugs may influence attraction, stimulation, and climax. All these factors are matters to discuss with physicians.

The idiosyncrasies of sex can be serious, but when exaggerated, they can become hilarious. Passion in conversation can become a plaything. The reversal of its significance in humans is a target of humor. Fun lovers and movie buffs went to see *Sex and the City*. Curiosity provoked reactions that went beyond liking or disliking the movie. The movie made quite a hit with young people, but one senior, with a bit of sarcasm in her voice, asked of another, "What makes them rave about this movie?"

"Young kids, yes, like ours—twenty, thirty, forty—aren't embarrassed about sex. They're open, even blatant and scintillating, about their sexuality. Look at the way they dress. They expose as much as they dare. If that isn't better advertising than a billboard, I don't know what is. They experiment with as much as they dare. And they're open and conversant about it. They don't whisper it in each other's ears, blush, and titter the way we did."

"What was so scintillating? I thought it was all about crude sex," retorted the first lady.

By now, the whole group was fired up. Another asked, "Did seniors find it scintillating?" The answer made eyes open wide.

Soon another voice was heard. "Some people are still stuck in the eighteenth century. I know of one woman, and this is the honest truth, who never showed her body to her husband. On their wedding night, she found her nightgown too revealing. She quickly reached for a needle and thread and sewed up the V in front so that chest and breast were concealed. And more than that, for over sixty years, she dressed and undressed in her closet."

"And the husband? He never rolled up her nightgown?"

"He was as sorely informed as she."

"Well, we surely didn't get maps from our parents. A little word here and there. The most I heard was 'Never say no to your husband.'"

Some honesty did come forth from another woman. "I'm glad I had a husband that at least learned from petting or whatever—still I can't say the f-word—but he found the sensitive areas and made me anticipate intercourse—there, I said it. I had a great sex life, and I miss it, and him, terribly."

And all this started from saying *scintillating*.

"Well, that movie does stimulate thought and conversation. Will you ever forget the scene when the gorgeous seductress bared the table, spread a fancy tablecloth, lay down, and decorated her body with appetizers on every sensitive spot on her body? Delectable any way you think about it! And she waited for her lover and waited and waited and waited hour after hour but lost the lust she started with and consumed the artichokes herself, one by one. By the time the lover arrived, she was a tearstained, unhappy gal. Think of that scene. Wow, It could be a metaphor for the whole sequence of courting days."

"That was supposed to be her Valentine's Day greeting."

"Yeah, speaks volumes about the stuff women take from men."

"Heck, she was imaginative!"

"To what end?" That remark prompted general laughter.

"Let's not go there. I like *scintillating* better."

"My son would have liked it, I'm sure." Nothing was stopping these women, who had learned about "all that stuff" through living the women's lib period.

"Learned 'all about that stuff' before it was too late, I hope. Sex has added flavor and pleasure to my life." With hearty laughter from all, which was its own way of confirming their lives, they made a break for the coffee ... and that culminated the discussion that day.

Dr. Jennifer M., gynecologist, shared related information and anecdotal material with me. "Women," she said, "are more complex than men, physiologically and emotionally. As they grow older, they tend to lose natural cervical lubrication. As a consequence, intercourse can cause irritation, leading to rejection and complications for the couple." She advises topical estrogen cream that allows the skin to stretch more; more internal lubrication is necessary for postmenopausal women. Patience is a good trait in achieving understanding of what affects each partner best. Seeking professional advice is high priority.

"One woman told me that she's a seventy-eight-year old woman who always hears her mother's influencing voice, 'Use it or lose it.' To keep her romance alive, once a month, there are candles on the table, massage lotion on his bread plate, and their favorite musical tapes playing softly. Viagra and K-Y Jelly worked for them."

Another story Dr. Jen told me was about an eighty-year old woman, widowed in her sixties, who rather belatedly decided life was not over for her and consulted a dating service. She was matched with a rather distinguished, well-dressed man. They proved congenial, and she decided to try sexual intercourse with him. After a short time of dating, she began to feel irritation and pain. Embarrassed to go alone to the doctor, she asked him to escort her. They'd appeared to be a fine couple. He settled into a chair in the waiting room. She, in her dignified manner, smiled at others as she went into the doctor's office.

The doctor did not have good news for her: the doctor found genital herpes, a transmitted disease. As she walked out, infuriated by the doctor's analysis of her trouble, she raised her umbrella and came down on her lover's back with full fury.

In all honesty, shouldn't he have been straightforward about his condition, used condoms as a mutual consideration, or refrained from intimate sex? There is more on this topic later in the text.

With Viagra widely used, it would seem that women's liberation took another step forward. Sex was once again an option—and without fear of pregnancy to boot! But doctors warn about possible risks in senior sexual relationships. STDs (sexually transmitted diseases) should make you stop to weigh sexual freedom against your certainty that both partners are free of contractual disease. Doctors emphasize that sexual venture without protection is folly. Better to be safe than sorry. And better still is having the courage to question one another about sexual history.

Lies are like ants. Don't give them food; they will act like bears on a hunt for honey.

Esther C. Gropper

As we grow and evolve, developmental intelligence
is expressed in the deepening
qualities of wisdom, judgment, perspective, and vision.

—G. D. Cohen, M.D., *The Mature Mind*

Romance and Sex

> I write the whole year through
> Note after note to you, Too many, it may be
> To catch unfailingly
> The mood I would express
> But would you have them less?
> Shall I but once a year
> Declare that you are dear?
> Take for its worth each writing
> The impulse is too inviting.

*I*f you think writing this to a woman of eighty-eight years incredible, consider the above as one of many submitted to me by various residents for this project or for shared readings. And then think of your children when they were ten or so. Would they believe their parents are having sex? Could they picture their grandparents having sex?

Let me reassure you: some sexual stereotyping about seniors will always persist. The reality of it is elderly people may be having more sex, and of a better quality, than thought. According to a recent study from the AARP (American Association for Retired Persons), half of Americans over sixty engage in sex once a week or more. Protective potion, please!

Seniors tell researchers they don't believe they are too old for sex, because even with difficulties that age brings on, the desire for intimacy doesn't necessarily fade with time. In fact, for many, the need for affection and contact becomes more important as prostate problems develop. Closeness becomes comforting and reassuring, lending importance to the male persona. Many men who have philandered in the past find their wives more important to them than ever. Too advanced in years to attract young chicks, they seek intimacy with their wives. And as an aside, if illness strikes such a man, he becomes dependent upon his wife for care. Her pillow next to his paradoxically gives him comfort and strength—and it could be vice versa. Let's be honest, women too have had their flirtations and then returned to stoke the banked flames with renewed interest.

I'm finding humor from seniors whenever baited. Ever in that residual sex cove in the brain are quips and double entendres. One afternoon, a man rose from the lunch table saying, "I'm going for my mail."

In response to which another quip emerged from the cove: "I'd rather go for my female."

Of course, such exchanges raise smiles. Some may label the men as "lecherous dirty old men" but seniors don't put a label on it. They don't think themselves too old to share what comes naturally. The desire for intimacy doesn't fade with time.

It is that shared closeness that bereaved feel the most. The reassuring bodily warmth of a hug is the affirmation of life and love. Many a second marriage is the search for closeness, of a companion to love and be loved. To quote one eighty-nine-year-old man, "Without that, life is worthless, useless. I wanted to die when my wife died. Life's obligations were over. My life was empty. My gun was already loaded. My family recognized my intention, sold my house and wares, and arranged for my moving to a senior residence. One afternoon, at a bridge game that hardly held my attention, I looked up and saw the bluest eyes across the room. The smiling eyes welcomed me to a total surprise. I cannot believe I met someone who introduced me to a second chance at romance. I haven't stopped grieving, but there is an overlay of pleasure that is easing my pain, showing me another life to enjoy. To me, it is miraculous. When I hold her in my arms and feel the warmth of her body against mine, I regain the meaning of life. I feel a love, an intensity of feeling that is strangely new and familiar to me. Every love lyric has new awareness for me. Every smile brightens my life. If she is late coming down for dinner, old feelings obsess me: I've lost her; she's gone. Then I see her turn the corner, bright-eyed and looking for me. I'm spinning into my new world."

His new world is fraught with optimism. "When I think of spending at least five years with you, sitting with you at dinner, seeing your eyes twinkle with affection, sharing stories of our lives, laughing or shedding a tear at past experiences, shopping with you and seeing you in clothes that so become you, of going to theater, movies, concerts—all the things my life hungers for, holding your hand, dancing with you, sharing news, books—keeping up with the world with someone that shares interests with me—my miracle glows. She has given me a new life, a rich life when I had thought a bullet would end my misery. Do you understand that a ninety-year-old feels this way?"

As for the younger people, they might smirk when they hear their buddies talk about hearing their parents' beds creak or laugh when something is mentioned about Grandma's companion whose paws are all over her. She's sexy? The thought is ludicrous, far-fetched. Young people have no idea nor understand the lifelong and lifeline role of sexuality and intimacy. Sex talk is common among adolescents and seniors. One is anticipating; don't think the other is solely reminiscing.

New ways of living and sharing are common on the senior scene. This is one time when history reverses itself. Senior patterns are predicated on the examples set by younger generations. Couples move in together for the same reasons: sharing chores, pillow talk long missed, cozy sleeping, and getting up with a smile because there's someone to look at and talk to over breakfast. And don't minimize the factor of financial savings from sharing an apartment. These funds can be used on pleasurable activities and trips.

Some find living together this way seductive, but finalize it with marriage. Is that too complicated legally? Is there security in living together as is? The choice is yours.

Esther C. Gropper

**When passion awakens,
You become young in heart
And dance again.**

—J. O'Donohue

Fun-Loving Seniors

How older people react to queries about age:
"I'm sixty-five, plus some months."
"How many?"
"246."
How's that for attitude?
"How old are you?"
"I'm in my eighties."
It was an honest answer. Eighty-nine is still in the eighties.
"You don't mean that. You're kidding. You can't be."
"But I am."
"What's kept you so youthful? Alive?" He struggled for the right word.
"Listen carefully: I'm good in bed." How's that for maintaining an image?

You can view the progress of age with some humor. You could stand back and look at yourself and smile or fret, but your mood might be lighter if you recall George Carlin's references to aging. Do you realize that the only time in our lives when we liked to get old was when we were kids? If you were less than ten years old, you were so excited about aging that you thought in fractions.

Do you know another time when people are proud to give their age? When they are in their nineties. They then will tell you how many years to their one hundredth birthday. If they don't, someone else provides the data. "We'll celebrate Selma's 100th in two years."

You may want to read the entire piece by going online. I'm skipping to ages that are pertinent:

You *get into* your eighties, and every day is a complete cycle: you *hit* lunch; you *return* four thirty; you *reach* bedtime. And it doesn't end there. Into the nineties, you start going backward: "I *was just* ninety-two."

Then a strange thing happens. If you make it over one hundred, you become a little kid again: "I'm one hundred and a half!"

May you all make it to a healthy one hundred and a half! Wondering how?

Start Your Day:
1. Look in the mirror with a smile and a wink. You've made it to another day. Make it a good one.
2. Does the scale look at you with scorn? Get back on the bed and do stretch exercises.
3. A warm shower, especially hot, if you can take it, on aching spots. A good rub and then
4. Dress as if you have or could expect an invitation to lunch. Looking good makes you feel good.
5. Put a little make up on – subtly – a highlight to the eyes; shadow out some of the wrinkles. A cosmetician can help you do it expertly. Shy about it? My aging mother-in-law used to say, "A little powder and a little paint makes a woman what she ain't."
6. Posture! Erect! It gives you elegance, the kind you can't buy. If you use a walker, step forward between handles; hold the handles lightly. Do you remember how proudly you pushed your baby carriage.? Try that same attitude now.
7. Eat a healthful breakfast. In fact, every meal should have daily requirements for energy and managed weight. Dorothy F., a resident, said, "After all, age, weight, height are numbers and mine are not listed."

8. Check your diary. What do you have planned for the day? Every day should have something new to learn and adds to your pleasure: a walk in the park, a lecture, an exercise class? The Library that has good programs and you could check out a good book or film.
9. Feel like an afternoon nap? A good idea. I once asked an 85 year old family friend (when I was 25) what kept her so beautiful. Her answer: I had three lively boys. When they napped, I did, too. It gave me patience for the rest of the day.
10. Laughter is wonderful exercise. Internet provides enough humor to share over lunch or dinner. Paul comes to the Kaffee Klatch with print outs of choice comments from Internet. Those are my guidelines. I hope they help make your day great!

And always remember:

Life is not measured by the number of breaths we take but by the moments that take our breath away.

Esther C. Gropper

The mystery of life is not a problem to be solved
but a reality to experience.
– Anonymous

Dealing with Problems

The secrets of our behavior can be tracked now to specific areas in the brain. In many research centers around the world, scientists are examining, observing, and finding particular areas of the brain, highlighting and recording where the brain is engaged, and then estimating the amount and intensity of brain activity.

How effectively do people handle stress, anxiety, over-scheduling, fear? Some can handle despondency because they have emotional strength and understand the pitfalls of retiring from social interaction. They know that secluding themselves isolates them, and that one good way to prevent depression is to join what a group is doing. That leads to distraction, an effective way to rest your concerns and perhaps return to them with a quieter mind. A good way to lift your spirits is to seek activities outdoors: jogging, walking, swimming. Give the overburdened part of the brain a break.

I was seriously depressed after years of caring for an Alzheimer's patient and actually suffering injuries trying to help him up from falls. The repetitive questions, the long periods of silence, and the childlike behavior wore down my energies. I had doubts about myself and felt guilty because I might not be doing enough for him. I recognized the symptoms of depression I was feeling and sought help. For people who are immobilized by their emotions, professional aid should be the first port of call.

It is time to seek professional help when you feel stress is affecting your health. Be alert to the warnings: When it seems as if troubles will never end; when you feel depressed, sad, and tearful; when life does not seem to be worth living; when you lose your appetite; when you have difficulty sleeping; when you find yourself turning to alcohol or smoking excessively; and when you feel clamped up and can't talk because you're overwhelmed by worries of helplessness, don't think there's no one or nothing to help you out of your abysmal situation. You can reach out to any source I've mentioned or consult your local government agencies.

As a final note on assistance: If you find yourself a victim of elder abuse—physical, emotional, and psychological slurs, harassment, improper use of your funds or property, or coercion into signing documents you don't understand or any financial exploitation—or if you find signs of unwelcome sexual advances, do yourself a favor and call an elder abuse hotline, or 911 if it's an emergency. Don't overlook checking credit card and bank statements. You don't want to become a victim of identity theft. I am indebted to Sunny Sussel for this information. Sunny has served over ten years with the Area Agency on Aging.

If you find yourself in the role of a caretaker, you will hear about distractions as an aid to healing painful feelings. Unquestioningly, it is the way to go. I urge you to break the chain of sadness—not by watching TV for hours or by listening to radio talk shows and engaging in other sedentary activities, but by choosing active pastimes: volunteering for theaters, hospitals, community groups. Retired lawyers become advocates for the poor and helpless, AmeriCorps, and Caring Connections. Join volunteer respite programs and earn vouchers for continuing education—a nice reward for those who ached for a college education. It is never too late to sign up for college. You read about ninety-year-olds getting degrees. If you dreamed about attaining a degree, go for it!

Volunteers facilitate with language and computer skills and assist in easing students into classes; RSVP serves over two hundred volunteer stations that include many not-for-profit organizations; We Care programs serve hospitals, sheriff's departments, theaters, public schools, transportation-assistance programs, and meet many more needs, not the least of which are food and support problems, or isolation and family indifference.

Happy hour at our residence, and possibly yours, is real bait for the person wading in shallow waters.

"What keeps the flow?" a resident asked me.

Flow? That had to be bar-scene jargon. Did that refer to swimming with the tide? Did it refer to being in with a crowd or seeking to get in with a crowd—of peppy people, of course?

I took a jab at the latter thrust. "People gather at art-gallery openings and organized biking, walking, jogging, or hiking groups. Consider local excursions." Every part of the country offers scenic and unusual sites. Local libraries today feature topical as well as literary discussions. Workshops for handiworks for men as well as women, choral groups, drama readings, and writing workshops are offered at community centers. Check your local newspaper for details.

Evenings empty and blue? Change your attire and ask about local dance offerings: folk, tango, rumba, ballroom, square-dancing. All are available. Check them out. Just be part of something active. Serendipity is part of the game. You never know who is coming in your direction.

I remember when I was fifty, widowed, and visiting in Florida. I attended a Brandeis University literature class. I chose that because it is my field of interest. The professor gave a new twist to an old story that prompted me to ask questions and to air my interpretation, amicably received and added to by others. After the session, a well-groomed, smiling woman approached me. "You sound informed." After a few more exchanges, she asked me to lecture for the Brandeis Ladies in her county.

My own activities widened, and a wonderful friendship developed between us. This is a good example of how to dip into your fountain of knowledge and self-regard. Since seniors often find themselves in new communities, they would be wise—and wisdom is the soul's natural food—to put their best foot forward and reveal something of themselves to others. People are curious about new people in their neighborhoods and about potential prospects near them. If you're fearful or not sure you're able to make that first step, take a few minutes with a pencil and paper and jot down ten reasons why someone might like to know about you. Reluctant? Sit there until one factor comes forth: *I make personal greeting cards.* Another: *I enjoy aerobics.* Another and another. Soon you will have more than ten and be able to say, "Hey, I'd like to know a person like that!"—and mean it!

I haven't met a person yet whose life's course wasn't intertwined with the world's course of events. When I met Mort Weiss, he was occupied daily with visiting the wife of a friend he had known since age ten. In subsequent talks with Mort, I learned that he had been an only child who grew up in a household where parents, relatives, and friends always gathered and talked about politics and economics. Personally, Mort was more intrigued with the Yankees baseball team, but the family discussions had their impact. War talk prevailed in the late thirties, and Mort knew he would end up in the army and was convinced he would die young.

Into his late eighties, he laughs, and he laughs easily, at his early apprehensions. However, he did flirt with the possibility when he volunteered for a special assignment. (He felt he wasn't doing much as a teletype operator.) The special assignment was to find an antidote for mustard gas. The volunteers were subjected to six drops of mustard gas: three drops on each forearm. The army recorded any physical or mental changes. Fortunately, Mort does not recall any damage and acknowledges that the results of the experiment were not shared with the soldiers. He did say that fifty years later, he received a follow-up call from an army official who questioned him about his current health.

That same inherently principled man held sacred the request—the dying request of his forty-nine-year-old childhood friend Rudy—to take care of his wife, Ethel. Mort had been recently widowed himself, his wife succumbing to the prolonged, devastating effect of Alzheimer's disease. Mort prevailed upon Ethel to take an apartment in the same senior residence, just down the hall from him. Not too long after, Ethel suffered a stroke and was left with no cognitive connection on the right side of her brain. There is no more attentive person than Mort to her every need, patiently helping where needed, providing recreation and entertainment for her. Such devotion and consideration are admirable. Devotion among seniors is what we most often see with a disabled partner.

As a closing note, let me share what Mort said about his father. "My father was a wise and witty man. When I asked him about the success he had in life, he gave me one of his many aphorisms: Keep chopping the wood. Chop! Chop! Chop! But don't get lost in the sawdust."

I'd vouchsafe that every life bears indelible memories, moments of tear-dwelling pride. I think of my friend Lucille, who gave birth to four sons, the latter two twins. Mark, the oldest, matured in the rebellious sixties. His first job as a teacher was in a New York City grade school. He wasn't that many years apart from his fifth-grade students, and his approach to life still demonstrated childlike abandon. Distinction, please: he was not childish, but he possessed the inner joy of youth. He wanted to have the children know that education was fun, that you could greet the day at school with puzzles on the board that tricked you into liking math, and that hangman games could make spelling amusing. And Mark dressed in jeans and T-shirts with artful proverbs and songs.

The trouble began with Mark's dress code. The principal didn't like it and thus wrote notes to Mark about proper attire. She wrote him notes about methodology outlined in curriculum materials. Mark wrote back that his methods were more appropriate for learning what schools teach and proved it to her by grades; his apparel, if anything, encouraged reading, writing, and arithmetic. The principal had no patience for what she termed an "unprincipled teacher." She dismissed him with unfavorable statements that precluded being placed in another school.

Mark went to Hawaii, lived in a tree house, met another rebel from the states, lived with her, and had two children with her that have grown up as fine citizens. Mark acclimated to an island that was relaxed in atmosphere and culture. He became involved in the cultural life of the state, became a sports announcer, and went on to do many favorable jobs for the government. He and the mayor had a very cordial relationship. He had very favorable ties to his family, visiting the States whenever one of his brothers could afford to send him a ticket. His children visited the families as well.

After what would be a considerable lifetime of changes, Lucille made one of her visits to the island, the occasion being her ninetieth birthday. Lucille is one of the rare nonagenarians with unmatched verve and vigor. The mayor, Billy Kenoi, impressed with Mark and his mother, proclaimed May 30, 2009—her actual ninetieth birthday—as Lucille Rosenthal Day in Hawaii County. Here is a copy of the proclamation:

COUNTY OF HAWAII

Proclamation

WHEREAS, Lucille Edna Isaacs was born in Brooklyn, New York on May 30, 1919; and

WHEREAS, with the aid of a handsome Bronx boy, Irving Joseph Rosenthal, they brought forth four boys into this world; Mark Alan (aka Rosey), David Lee, and the twins Gary Andrew and Glen Michael; and

WHEREAS, Lucille and Irv raised four wonderful boys with grace, humor, quality home cooking, love and most of all patience; and

WHEREAS, everyone is better for knowing lovely Lucille, her friends, neighbors, bowling teammates, bridge and mahjong players, and particularly her children and grandchildren; and

WHEREAS, Lucille continued to work as a bookkeeper into her 80s in order to have extra money to buy things for her grandchildren; and

WHEREAS, Lucille is one of those rare individuals who captures the hearts of all those that come into contact with her; and

WHEREAS, Lucille's kind and selfless spirit, her love (Tiger Woods) and determination, have created this beautiful human being; and

WHEREAS, Lucille is such a medical marvel that at ninety she has to prove she's not taking any medication; and

WHEREAS, as a testimony to a life well lived, Lucille's only regrets are that her beloved husband didn't get to share in all the joy, and that she didn't take up golf sooner;

NOW, THEREFORE, I, BILLY KENOI, Mayor of the County of Hawai'i, do hereby proclaim May 30, 2009, as

LUCILLE ROSENTHAL DAY

in the County of Hawai'i and urge all citizens to be inspired by Lucille Rosenthal, in honor of her 90th birthday, a significant milestone in her magnificent life.

IN WITNESS WHEREOF, I have hereunto set my hand and caused The Seal of the County of Hawai'i to be affixed. Done this 30th day of May, 2009, in Hilo, Hawai'i.

Billy Kenoi
Mayor
County of Hawai'i

Esther C. Gropper

**There is no cage for love.
There is one for negativity.
You can almost hear the clang of the prison door
closing in on you.
– Source Unknown**

Re-channeling Emotions

On wounded feelings:

Unlike the natural openings in the body, a wound is an unexpected foreign opening. It is a place where the sealed surface that keeps the interior hidden is broken. A wound is also, therefore, a breakage that lets in light and a sore place where much of the hidden pain of the body surfaces. Some accident or dark intention forced the breakage of surface. A wound awakens and focuses the reserve of the immune system, the overriding desire of the body is to seal the opening, to heal and restore the inner darkness, yet the wound takes its time to heal. While the wound is open, new light flows into the helpless dark and the inner night of the body weeps through the wound. In the rupture and pain it causes, a wound breaks the silence. It cries out. It ruptures through the ordinary cover of words we put on things. Each wound has its own unique shape and signature. Woundedness is one of the places where normal words and descriptions break down. We know the distance words have to travel whenever we attempt to tell someone of the pain we feel. It is no wonder that the wound as a sore point of vulnerability cries out for some new form in which to express itself.

The beauty that emerges from woundedness is a beauty infused with feeling. This is a beauty that has suffered its way through the ashes of desolation until the words or music emerged to equal the hunger and desperation at its heart.

Most woundedness remains hidden, lost inside forgotten silence. Indeed, in every life there is some wound that continues to weep secretly.

Even after years of attempted healing, the woundedness can be refined into beauty. Wonderful transfiguration takes place; for instance, compassion is one of the most beautiful presences a person can bring to the world and most compassion is born of one's own woundedness. When you have felt deep emotional pain and hurt, you are able to imagine what the pain of others is like; their suffering touches you. This is the most decisive and vital threshold in human experience and behavior. The greatest evil and destruction arises when people are unable to feel compassion. The beauty of compassion continues to shelter and save our world. If that beauty were quenched, there would be nothing between us and the end—darkness would pour in torrents over us.

—John O'Donohue, *Anam Cara*

Anger

There are more synonyms for *anger* than for *affection*.

Direct negative thoughts to more positive ones.

Instead of, "I don't want to see that movie," try "I prefer seeing ... a great cast and ..."

Instead of, "That's not a good time for me," try "Wouldn't it be more convenient for all of us to meet at...?"

Anger is a human reaction to hurt pride and dignity.

Raise your eyebrows, not the roof.

What are some of the healthy ways of dealing with stress, anger, and fear? Suppose for a moment that your granddaughter (or grandson) is distraught because friends are trying drugs or drinking heavily. She tells you that she is being prodded, teased, or jeered at for not joining the fun. She is not looking for your attitude. She knows your bias, but she needs a way to handle the teasing or pressure. How will you answer the question? This is a challenge—an essay question on your final exam of life. What are you going to hand down? Keep in mind that your grandchild looks to you as a model. You will be graded (not by me) on how you handle, distinguish, and respect differences, and how you maintain a serious and sympathetic voice without sermonizing. Above all, responses should be without judgmental comments. Be assertive, rather than angry or judgmental. If this obvious question arises, be prepared.

I asked Dr. Magid, a psychologist, about this possibility. His answer was, "You have to start winning the battle, because he came to you for help. People came to me with this dilemma because things became a problem for them. At first, it was fun and easy to get the weed; then they found it was affecting their moods; they weren't thinking straight; their minds were cloudy, their judgment off course; their relationships were tearing apart. This was no longer a sweet, tender moment of growing up—of pre-teenagers curious about their first kiss or seeing Mom and Dad in bed locked in a sexual position. This wasn't about petting or ignoring permission to borrow the car. This was about drugs, because pot is an introduction to more harmful and addictive drugs."

What did you do to solve your own moral problems? Focus on the question that is not about ignoring permission to borrow a tie, a shirt, a dress, the car. Make two lists with the young person: One is to be the advantages (what he gains); give this list fair ground. The second list has the consequences (what he loses), and be not timid about adding to it. You're already informed and experienced; you don't have to show off your knowledge. He has to struggle through the mud, wipe off his shoes, polish up his act (a whole bunch of clichés, but you get the point) and decide on the path to follow.

Everybody has worth; you must find your own self-worth. Be determined and fearless; push everything to the hilt. What do you have to lose? You'll find your generation is charitable. Their concerns are much like yours or have moved on from that phase and can offer counsel. But don't expect or wait for someone to fix things for you. That part is your responsibility.

The road you follow can become less fretful, less stressful as you become aware of your natural abilities. You were gathering knowledge to smooth the sharp corners. You have to get credits for that. You'll get that degree in lifelong learning with just a few more observations of inward and outward behavior. One of the snags is loneliness. Or should I call it an enemy to our contentment?

**All Man's history is an endeavor to shatter his loneliness.
—George W. Shaw**

Loneliness

Can you fall in love at eighty? Eighty-five? Ninety? Is that speed dating? After all, the clock has ticked away many more years than you have ahead. Some men (women, too) are more aggressive in their desire to have a relationship before the final sleep.

One woman told of sitting in the auditorium when a friend came in and sat in back of her. While greeting the friend casually, she observed her with a man. That was not unusual; where they lived, the culture included a disposition to informal mingling. But this man, evidently a newcomer and anxious to meet residents, asked her name and followed the question up by asking her to have dinner with him. She thought it rude to ask that when he was in company with a woman. After the performance, he directed the question to her again. He lost no time in calling.

She was reluctant; his manners were open to question. As time passed, she did dine with him. Leaving the dining room, he asked to walk with her to her door. Reconciling his error, he was courtly as they walked to her apartment. He asked to come in. She demurred. Yes, of course in subsequent meeting, he persisted, assuring her that he would not do anything that she did not favor. He told her often how much he desired a relationship, whatever that entailed—though he never defined what he meant by "relationship" and said little to describe his intent. He urged her to let him massage her feet, all the time telling her how beautiful she was.

She recognized her inward signals of disinterest, and she suggested other ladies to call. This sounds like a service being set up, but in reality, she was as delicate as she could be. She did persuade him to seek out another companion.

The experience made her wonder about her negative responses. Her wounds were still tender after caring for her late husband. That led to sincere questions. Could she have a male companion without intimacy? Did she want another involvement? Such are the uncertainties we must resolve.

The question was brought up at a subsequent session of "What's On Your Mind?" Bluma pointed out that some men and women lived in separate apartments but were together during the day, having meals together and attending events together; others lived together; and marriages had occurred in the years she was living here. Answers would come when the questioner met someone who became important to her.

This topic is too important to gloss over. In fact, it was *the* question in the minds of many who feel loss or have severed a relationship. Dr. Rollo May, who has served on the faculty at Harvard and Yale, tells us that the feeling of loneliness and emptiness go together. In a period of traumatic change, people become aware that conventional desires and goals they have been taught to pursue no longer bring them any security or give a sense of direction. He or she looks around for other people to give them a sense of direction, or at least comfort in the knowledge that he or she is not alone in fright; thus two phases are experienced of the same basic problem of anxiety. Healing time is important. The inner you will sense a deeper need and reach out for affection with its own innate signals.

Don't bemoan your singleness; instead, revel in your singularity.

Stormy Weather

My forty-five-year-old-sister was embarrassed by the untoward attention she was getting from male friends. She was concerned that this would harm her marriage, a good marriage. She implored me to give her a reason for the unsolicited and improper advances.

"Do I have an animal smell, a pheromone that excites men? Am I doing something I'm not conscious of?"

"No," I answered seriously, "unless it's the scent of elegance, Trudy. You have an aura about you that distinguishes you from others. Your vitality, carriage, and sparkling eyes are like fluorescent lights. They tell people you are an exciting, intelligent woman, and you are a bright conversationalist. Women are awed as well as men."

She confided to me that she felt shame, as if she had been doing something sinful. It was a feeling that women get after they've been raped. They try to understand what provoked it, end up seeing themselves as provocative walking sex symbols, and take the blame. Change has come about for women who are encouraged to understand their powerless inclinations.

Developmental change has to occur in other phases of our social and marital relationships. We have to be participants in a process toward clarity of feelings and reasons. You may wish you had thought out, talked out, or worked out knots before they became so entangled that divorce, separation, or rejection was the only escape route ahead. I wonder at times which was best answer: the one in which the woman faced with unfaithfulness chose divorce—*How could you do this to me and your family* or the one who sought counsel and emotional recovery to reconnect to her spouse—*Where did we falter in our interactions that led to this?* Where the "me" shifted to "we," there was a better chance at productive dialogue. One answer doesn't fit all. I know of women who lived forgiveness, never reprimanding for a past sin, and went on

Dance until the Music Stops

to true family life and gratifying experiences. Others, filled with pride, could not forgive, sued for divorce, and spent years venting vitriol and spending sums of money over unwillingness to share assets and possessions. And some lived and accommodated to a life of sharing a spouse.

They never spoke of their lifestyle. They continued friendships when convenient, and they carried themselves with a dignity that foreclosed comments.

Most counselors will say that a true and sincere desire to restore a relationship yields good results and tighter bonds.

I have offered three choices. Younger couples don't have the wisdom of age. They have neither the experience nor knowledge for reaching best results. They are apt to rely on emotional knowledge. A good thing to keep in mind is that older people can offer comfort and advice.

In my own experience as a writer and counselor, I would present a dilemma that had several possible solutions. I often suggested acting or writing a story in which the main character is beset with a serious (designated) situation. Before writing, they were to rule three columns on a planning page with headings for an Impulsive Reaction (reliance on instinctive responses), Emotional Reaction (strong feeling evoked that led to action), and Reasoned Response (relying on known facts and feelings). This writing nurtured problem-solving skills. I adapted this format from my counseling experience. I like making lists because it sorts out thoughts, makes you search your mind, and offers a study sheet for decisions.[6]

Anecdotes are remarkable for their appropriateness. I share this one that will make any couple want to find the underlying message:

Dr. Frank Magid, psychologist, offered this metaphorical view of a good marriage: Two porcupines on a freezing-cold hill in winter have a problem. How can they cling together, close enough to keep each other warm, yet far enough apart that they don't scratch each other's

---

6 Dr. D. Goleman offers a comparable approach.

eyes out? Solution: they had to find the optimal distance—the perfect distance—between them.

In marriage, each partner usually has a different distance for comfort. What is too close for one may be too far apart for the other. Solution: experience before or after the wedding reveals each one's comfort zone. Love is willingness to accommodate to each other's comfort.

To obtain a sense of comfortable distance when treating troubled couples, the family therapist may ask them to walk slowly toward each other. Each is asked to say when the other is too close for maximum comfort. Suggestion: try it. And, obviously, *distance* includes *time*.

Anger is never without reason, but seldom a good one.
—Benjamin Franklin

Recommended for disappointments and for healing a rift in your relationship:

Are you face-to-face with a sullen face?
Has your lover turned cold?
Is there a common complaint between you?
I will risk saying this latter guess is glaring at you. It might be worth the effort to explore whether one or both is harboring a chronic complaint. Sometimes, when silence exists, distance gets wider and sets you far apart. Remember the story of the porcupines? Even they know what is the right distance that's good for couples.

While I know of no physical exercise to span the distance, except for using your mouth, there is the danger that anger will spurt instead of words that offer reconciliation. So, hold your tongue and use your head. Let your mind serve you before your tongue lashes out. Turn your mental directory to soothing words. You just might remember something happily mated people say. Difficult as it may be, they are frank with each other. They ask each other what they like in sexual play. One of you may be naive and be surprised by what can turn a man or a woman on. One or the other should know the erotic pressure points; if not, get thee to the bookstore or Internet. Have a good time learning together.

When this point was reached in one of our table talks, I suggested others share their best technique, but one woman was curious about this open response.

She asked another, "Does your husband try something new? Does he say he loves you, just like that? Does he bring you flowers once in a while?"

"No, he forgets. Sometimes I want to ask him how he can forget. I say something silly like, 'If you loved me, you'd remember.' When that kind of answer pops up, I laugh. It's so corny, so Grade-C movie scenario, and it comes out in light mockery that makes us both laugh, because one of us will remember a sexologist who chided the advice given by friends. "Don't ever say no"—that was what your grandmother told your mother, and what your mother told you. The modern gal will say, "How about a practice passion session?" Or he will. And you're off in a lighter mood and with heightened interest in each other. Or be imaginative. Create your own concept of sexually arousing play. Have a code word: *Adagio*? *Foreplay*? Stir up your relationship every once in a while, or you'll find yourself trying another bed mate with no history of the good things you shared with your former playmate."

"The other day, Valentine's Day," shared another woman, "I was in the market and, by coincidence, was near the flower display. I was truly amazed to see a cluster of men critically choosing a plant or bouquet for his spouse or companion. I wished I could have snapped a picture of one man holding an orchid plant aloft as if he were presenting it to a woman on a pedestal. I don't care if it's a Hallmark reminder that did it. The result mattered."

If you're in the aging stage, arousal comes latently. Why not revert to courtship days, when a gift was flowers or chocolates or a book the other expressed an interest in reading. Men love that expression of appreciation. I have no measure of comparison, but I wonder how such gestures rate against Viagra. I do know Viagra or other penile enhancement drugs have a 45 percent rate of success. You have to think of alternatives for the 55 percent balance. My good friend Judy Braunfeld, a notable gerontologist in Champaign, Illinois, tells her clients to consider mutual masturbation. Now, that shouldn't need definition at this stage of your life! It's foreplay you were adept at way back in your youth; now it's master-class skill at this action/art that rocks the boat. Ms Braunfeld also shared a neat verse with me:

> Love is a drug
> New love is like cocaine
> The high rarely lasts.

That sums up one alternative. There might be more gratification in the seduction of a cooled lover. Let me share another piercing reminder of showing and preserving affection, this from my wise, well-versed friend Bob.

As a young child in Austria, Bob's friend felt a deep love for his horse. He never went out without stopping at the barn to rub the nose of his horse and whisper that he loved him. The horse acknowledged the affection with nodding of his head. One day, he was invited to join a game of marbles by his neighboring friends, who urged him to hurry. He felt compelled to stop at the barn, but he gave the horse a quick pat on his head. The horse did not nod in return, and he never did after that, despite the many attempts the boy made to show his affection. Does a horse have enough intelligence to interpret a lapse of affection as betrayal? Did a change in affection or loyalty cause the horse to change his response? This is an example of animal nature, so approximate to human nature that it bewilders us.

Esther C. Gropper

Age
Old age will fly kites of past dreams
and tie long ribbons to flutter—
to test their paper wings among the clouds.
The winds, no longer strong, flag their spines;
the strings, no longer taut, flay their minds
but the spirit that swayed
a thousand minds or more
will ever soar—ever soar.

e.c.g.

Choice Is Everything

The questions persisted: How to establish a more favorable view of the senior years? What made the difference? Why were some people cheerful and companionable, and others looked as if they carried the weight of the world? Why was someone like Helen W. able to carry her grief over the loss of two children through continued decades of her life while still creating beautiful paintings and unique beading? She worked with Selma F., also creatively endowed, on musicals and performances at the residence. They were two single women who always had a cheerful smile and conversation!

Victor Borge would have said, "The difference between you and me is a smile!" Way back in the thirties, someone wrote in my class book, "I'd walk a mile to see her smile!" Was it early acknowledgment of affability? Did someone turn off the spigot of cheer for the sad ones? Or was there something else—a crisis—that prompted change and adaptation beneficial? What in early history set the pattern?

After having read the review of *Gulf Stream* by Poet Laureate Robert Pinsky, I had the pleasure of attending his reading at the Chautauqua Institute. He offered us his most valuable contribution of contemporary poetry's necessity and vitality: how poetry speaks from the heart and mind. This short poem is worth sharing:

> Deciding to remember
> And what to remember
> Is how we decide who we are.
> I am a creature of shame
> I am ashamed to say

One woman in the class asked an intriguing question: "Is a spontaneous thought then selected?"

"Now that's something to ponder for yourself," said the poet. "I gave you my thought."

I always wondered why I recoiled from sharing memories. Most of my friends talked glowingly, nostalgically, about childhood experiences. I was always ashamed. I grew up in shame, carrying shame in all I did. I backed away from engaging. I was always expecting questions about my childhood and values derived from them. Pinsky's statement touched me to the core.

As for ancestors, I had no maternal guidance other than from my grandmother, and I overstated her role. She visited sporadically when needed; the need came when Mama had a breakdown. In between her hospital treatments, there was the darkness a paranoid person lives in. Grandma was kindness itself. As I grew up, she was my ideal, but one of a different European culture. Of course I could conjure up idyllic recollections to put on the scale. I guess those were selected memories—or fabrications that haunted me with their dishonesty.

Why was I always aware of fabrications? Because I did pretend a different life, and I knew that my imagined one was impressive. What could I pride myself in? What would make me belong? It was years later that I gained insight to my actions: we learn by what we like as well as from what we do not like.

Sadness trailed after that confession. Others seemed preoccupied with recent research on inner thoughts, just as I was. Outwardly, many women and men seem well poised, friendly, learned, and calmly sophisticated, but what about the hidden emotional baggage? Deprivations? Losses and sadness? How to alleviate the sadness? How did some people convert hardship to strength, whereas others succumbed to weakness? Could not their imaginations improvise for them, making believe as children so often do in their play? Later I learned the danger of living and sustaining life in an imaginary world, of having delusions of grandeur. These were questions I wanted to pursue. They prompted my search. The people I interviewed shared insights. But what is the psychological truth?

I found statements in the Readings* indicating that we're wired for optimism or pessimism, but we have the will to change, and that can lead to better goals.

Yes, that is one of the strong recommendations for our generation. We are gifted with more time to live. Why not make life close to your model concept of yourself? The risk is not serious. Change is constant. You can try on another mode that suits better. In fact, as you would choose an outfit from your closet for a certain occasion, choose a lifestyle that appeals to you right now, in this time of your life.

Change is everything.

* See Suggested Readings in back of book.

Esther C. Gropper

I want not only to be loved
But to be told I am loved.
The realm of silence is large beyond the grave.

—George Eliot

Know Thyself

Better goals have always played a part in maturation. You are the sum total now of how you achieved your present position. Do you like your way? Does it bring you satisfaction? Do you know why you now react the way you do? If so, help others to see and share your view. You don't like it? You still have control and time to change.

Psychologists have been trying to determine what it takes to lead life successfully. Dr. Salovey determines his basic definition along the lines of emotional intelligence in five domains that I share with you:

> **Knowing one's emotions.** Self-awareness—recognizing a feeling as it happens—is helpful. People with greater certainty about their feelings are better pilots of their lives.
>
> **Managing emotions**. Handling feelings so they are appropriate is an ability that builds on self-awareness. People who are poor in this ability are constantly battling feelings of distress, while those who excel in it can bounce back far more quickly from life's setbacks and upsets.
>
> **Motivating oneself.** Marshaling emotions in the service of a goal is essential for paying attention, for self-motivation and mastery, and for creativity. Emotional control—delaying gratification and stifling impulsiveness—underlines accomplishment of every sort. People who have this skill tend to be more highly productive and effective in whatever they undertake.
>
> **Recognizing emotions in others.** Empathy, another ability

that builds on emotional self-awareness, is the fundamental social skill. People who are empathetic are better at callings such as the caring professions, teaching, sales, and management.

Handling relationships. The art of relationships comprises, in large part, skill in managing emotions in others and social competence. These are the abilities that under gird popularity, leadership, interpersonal effectiveness, and so on.[7]

Your time spent thinking about your own emotional intelligence should give you insight to your own actions and reactions. There is succinct wisdom to ponder in the book by Daniel Goleman. One cannot overlook the virtues of humanity and love that kindle kindness and generosity, fairness and respect. Perhaps hardest of all to realize is that loving and allowing yourself to be loved is an ingredient of happiness.

---

7 Emotional Intelligence by Dr. Daniel Goleman

Esther C. Gropper

If your heart is a volcano,
how shall you expect flowers to bloom?
Khalil Gibran

Take responsibility for what you are and what you do.
Bring the best of things to others and receive the reflected joy.

—Buddhist thought

Learn to Fit In

I once heard ethnologist Dr. Wade Davis, author of *Book of Peoples of the World: A Guide to Cultures*, talk of his explorations in Ethiopia, where he met a bright young boy with tremendous potential. He envisioned this young boy in his Western mind and imagined what this boy could accomplish for himself and for his people if he had university education. When he broached the subject to the boy and his parents, the boy shook his head vehemently, saying "No! No! No! I won't go. I don't want to lose my color."

You can be sure there were many concerns besides displacement in his retort, to be summed up in *acculturation*. We really have little concourse with displaced people who have a history of ethnic or tribal wars, itinerants, or illegals filtering through our culture. We do not know their uncertainties, fears, and allegiances or what exposure, if any, they've had to the Western world. They are so out of touch with the rest of the world that they don't know how many foreigners would forfeit an eye to have their children acquire an education in the States.

In contrast, Dr. Peter Braunfeld and his family were refugees from Austria. His parents were intent upon giving their children a good education, not only to acculturate to them but to help them become accomplished citizens. True, they sought sanctuary from the anti-Semitism they were constantly dodging, but, as many in Nazi countries, they tried to judge the political climate and its impact on their lives. Eventually, they gave up their home, possessions, and business to come to the United States.

As an interim step, Peter was sent to England, as were many children in an attempt to save their lives. Peter was sent to Kings College in Somerset, run by the Church of England. A bright young man, he quickly learned the language and customs and did well scholastically. By coincidence, his roommate was Haile Selassie, who told Peter that he had spent many years living in a subway during the bombing of his country. The common thread was the search for refuge.

When Peter joined his family in Chicago, he was enrolled in a public school. He was there for a short time when the American children were anticipating the celebration of Thanksgiving. He was verbal child, and when the teacher cast him as a silent Native American, he asked why he couldn't be a Puritan, having a talking part instead of *ugh* or *mug*. The teacher didn't realize the irony in her reply: "You can't because you are English."

Peter recalls another school-play performance in which he was assigned the role of a shepherd in a nativity play. He had to provide the props. Instead of a shepherd's staff, he borrowed ski poles.

Despite these peculiarities and other stumbling blocks, his education brought him hope and stature in his professorial position at the University of Illinois at Urbana-Champaign. Peter, a world-renowned mathematician, became, through his theoretical papers, professor emeritus, invited many times to address university classes abroad. When you think of the people I have mentioned throughout this book, you see resolute people who adapted to a new culture and endowed it with their contributions to science, philosophy, mathematics, and creative arts. They changed their lives and the lives of others.

Esther C. Gropper

**Life is a ballet dance—
a glissade in the dance of love.
e.c.g.**

Life Is a Ballet Dance

"Dance me to the end of love ..."
—Leonard Cohen

At age eighty-eight, Evelyn Halper is still dancing, performing, lecturing, and giving classes in international dance history. Avidly involved in folk dancing by the time she was eighteen, she became interested in the origins of dance: why dance became intertwined with the culture and customs of peoples from the very beginning of civilization. When she lectures, she is factual as well as anecdotal and interpretative. Her body is always in dance mode.

Evelyn has taken workshops in ethnic dancing, so varied as to feature Russian/Ukrainian, Swedish, and Greek, as well as western European countries. Consequently, she has been a popular square-dance caller. Among her favorite dances are the Balkan favorites, Irish, Czech, Latvian, Lithuanian, and Israeli folk arrangements. She smiled when I asked about American folk dances.

"Yes," she said, "I remember teaching the Virginia Reel to a class of ten-year-olds." At that I laughed heartily, because my second husband, Barney, who acknowledged two left feet, could not master the Virginia Reel and had to stay after school to take further lessons until he had a passable rendition of the dance. To think, he graduated Harvard University magna cum laude without a high grade in dance!

With that, Evelyn told me that she was associated with a children's theater at one time and claimed children were her best audiences. El Burrito (The Donkey) was a huge success because the dance ends with the donkey rearing up against the master, jumping on the master and proving his *mastery*.

In the early years of television, she startled children with a tape of the dancing she had done at the Museum of the City of New York. (These tapes are part of a permanent collection now.) One child could not visualize how she could be on the screen and in their auditorium at the same time. "How did you get into the box each time you danced?"

I met Evelyn often at dance programs. We both marvel at the body movements of modern abstract acrobatic dance. Her comments always illuminate the choreography, gyrations, rhythms, and sounds of modern dance performances. Most significant, of course, is her continued participation in dance. At Palm Beach State College, she continues to teach, to entertain, and to enchant fans of folk dancing.

Esther C. Gropper

Happiness is the art of dreams: live the life you imagine.
—Henry Thoreau

Stay on the Happy Side

Dr. Ian K. Smith, author of *Happy,* raises the one question I always sought to answer. I ask this question in one form or another throughout this book. Why do some people turn out happy, while others labor through gloom and pessimism, even when the two groups were raised in similar circumstances?

I'd like to share these passages from the book:

> We are born optimistic creatures. It is our nature to overestimate the likelihood of positive events and underestimate the likelihood of negative events. Why do we do this? Research of the brain activity when people imagine positive events was bigger brain response that when they thought about negative events. Nature built our brain to see the glass half full. But what is not understood is why some still lean toward the pessimistic view of seeing the glass half empty. (There has been reference to happy babies as having been held lovingly by parents, food quickly provided and comfortably clothed.) The good view is that years of research have demonstrated that if you're not an optimist, you can learn how to be so.
>
> There are benefits in being optimistic. Optimists live longer, perform better, and face less stress; they are realists.
>
> So much of our time, our daily routines, is about doing what we need to do that has very little to do with the things we most enjoy. Carving out an hour a day, a paltry seven hours a week of 168 hours, seems to be an arduous task for many.

Do you know what the saddest response to that challenge was? "I don't know what I'd do with that hour."

Happiness can be derived from the simplest of things: reading a good book, visiting an art gallery or a museum, taking a leisurely walk, watching nature at play, watching a program you've wanted to see, or listening to favorite music.

My special hour is cocktail hour with Frank with good music in the background and pleasant conversation between us. Our yoga teacher says for her, it is early morning walking on the beach. For you, happiness may be the park, or an attractive mall, a place that perks you up and relaxes you. Be selfish for one hour; do what you want to do; dismiss what others might think. Make your own priorities. No one else will do it for you. Happiness is going for it. Get off the sidelines and get into the game.

Life is not meant to be a spectator sport but a spectacular event.

Finding your way through life and capitalizing on opportunities means a willingness to throw away fears and open your mind to the possibilities that populate your path to happiness. For some the penchant for search and discovery might be genetic. Some are more comfortable being risk averse. Or you just might yearn to be one that wants to live life to the fullest. Willing to take risks and not be discouraged. Some see the scenario and feel what the heck, the water may be cold, but it'll pump up the heart. Take the plunge.

Happy people exercise; exercise makes happy people.

Act and think Happy. You are what you think you are. After a while, acting happy takes on a reality and then you find—Happiness is Contagious.

New research on happiness tells us that even those prone to melancholy and grim temperament can lift their mood through a series of exercises and behaviors that are quite easy to accomplish: perform five acts of kindness a week. Of all the suggestions—and they all have to do with doing something for someone else—I like one the author mentions that I hadn't thought of: putting a coin in a meter for someone you don't know. Strengthen and deepen personal relationships.

The happiest people have close friends, strong family relationships, and romantic relationships—not the number, but the quality. A strong network is also associated with longer life.

Happy people also know how to forgive. As Aristotle said in *The Ethics,* "Remember, anyone can become angry—that is easy. But to be angry with the right person, to the right degree, at the right time, for the right purpose, and in the right way—that is not easy."

Life is full of renewals and opportunities, and how we embrace them gives our existence texture.

Dr. Ian Smith in *Happy* answers questions about optimism and pessimism by saying, "It wasn't until I started digging into research on the origins of happiness that I stumbled on part of the answer." (I have summarized or quoted points he makes that are meaningful and pertinent to the themes in this book.)

We're acquainted with differences in physiological characteristics, genes, but as for origins of happiness, we have to think in **happiness set points**. This is not to be equated with the high you get from a wished-for gift that's yours. Such bursts of happiness are temporary.

Eventually, you return to your level of set points. In one study, David Lykken concluded that 50 percent depended on genes and 50 percent on circumstances. Continued research narrows the latter to 40 percent controlled by your actions, with an additional 10 percent if you're lucky and good things happen to you.

Doesn't this equation offer hope that your input can make life better? Happier?

Of course, lower expectation translates into rarely being disappointed. The key is how well you control the impact of disappointment on your overall happiness. Some things you can't control, and of such situations you learn acceptance.

I have always taken commitments and promises seriously. I never said yes to my children to something I knew I couldn't make happen.

Esther C. Gropper

So it was with my first going-back-to-work teaching job in the New York City school system. The commute took me from one borough to the extreme end of another, through heavy commercial traffic cluttered with garbage trucks that stopped every other minute. Invariably, I arrived late and showed my frayed edges. My principal knew and understood, sat me down one day, admitted that my assignment was unfair, and explained that I could do nothing about the travail of travel I encountered and that I was to take it in stride until she could obtain a transfer for me that was better situated.

Blaming others comes easily but is as ineffective as depending on others for happiness. A critical component of happiness is being realistic. It's perfectly normal to feel mistreated or feel sad for good reasons. The key is how fast you can get through the bad mood without spilling over on others; then move on to more positive space.

After looking at records of how lottery winners improved their lives with cars, jewels, trips, bigger homes, and so on, it seems that a few years later they had returned to their previous lifestyles. Upon reflection, they liked activities such as long baths, going swimming, enjoying their fun playing games. hiking and picnics.

Is this true of retirees, after five years of tennis, golf, and luncheons? Gerontologists suggest that happiness becomes more sustained and has more of an impact because of characteristics surrounding the experience—meaning pleasure and engagement. Happiness is a crowded dinner table: friends and family sharing stories, laughs, opinions, and even good news and bad. What people want is good food, a big support group, and love and sharing. How would your list compare? Things you'd assume would bring happiness?

Check this list submitted by Dr. Smith:
Family, friends, social companionship
Helping others

Appreciating what you have; not feeling resentful
for what you don't have
Making a difference in someone else's life
Pursuing a passion
Taking pride in one's work
Forgiving someone for an offense and moving on
Not trying to keep up with the Joneses
If you have more valuable items to add, consider yourself a successful person.

- - - - -

With all that, isn't it more favorable to grow old at home?

I have made a strong case for retirement in an independent-living residence because I believe that community living offers sociability. One never need feel lonesome or rejected by society, and there are people to chat with at several interludes of the day.

You can have your privacy in your own apartment with your own furnishings and with your own mementos that keep love flowing.

Some meals are provided, if not all of them, and your apartment is equipped to hold provisions. Kitchens have refrigerators, stoves, and cupboards. Or dine out occasionally—try anything that keeps boredom at bay.

If you don't drive, transportation is available to doctors, shopping centers, theaters, and other places. You don't have to be a shut-in dependent upon Meals On Wheels or social aides.

Programs of social and intellectual content are offered every day. You don't have to wither in body or brain.

Physical maintenance and special exercise programs are generously provided in good residences. Most of them have good walking paths, fitness centers, dance and exercise classes, and activities on all levels of interest and capability. You can keep trim and healthy.

A multitude of other activities are offered according to financial and physical abilities. Investigating before making a decision is strongly advised.

Having said all this and offered intimate insights to life in a caring residence, it would be fair to submit the arguments for living and aging at home. I submit the substance (I hope) of a new book titled *Happiness Is Growing Old at Home* by Maria Tadd. This is a carefully documented work.

Living at home is less costly—in some cases substantially, depending on the choice of residence. Using her data, the national average of $19 an hour for a certified nursing aide would cost $20,748 for one year—about $16,000 less than at an assisted-living residence and $52,000 less than a nursing home. These prices may differ in areas. But the home has to be elder-user friendly; kitchen and bath appliances may have to be changed to make them accessible by wheelchair or walker. Meals On Wheels, visiting nurses, and other helpers might be needed to look in frequently. The resident might require assistance in going outdoors or to the stores.

Most important is being aware and making provisions for senior safety and security.

> Ms. Todd recommends the following:
> Make sure the home is safe:
> Stair treads secure
> Frayed carpet edges sheared
> Flooring, throw rugs, showers outfitted for safety (handles on bathtubs and showers) Furnishings without sharp edges
> Stairs well lighted, night lights installed, and so on
> Medical alerts set up, doctor visits scheduled
> Balance issues resolved (yoga can build resistance to falling)
> Diet carefully provided
> Companionship available

The author recommends contacting the Center for Disease Control for complete information. But you will discover, along the way, that new devices are constantly coming into the market.

One example, a new high-tech shirt that detects falls and sends computer messages to relatives, a panic button, whistles, and sensors are available. For more information, contact the Center for Aging Technology

Those who can manage motorized robots might want to know that they are nearing perfection and production. They will be remarkable tools to help the homebound. Electronic doorstops and magic carpets designed to help the elderly avoid falls are promising, as are shoes that send messages of imbalance and falls. Amazing new robotic devices will aid, remind, track medication, and direct while performing just about every precautionary action. Can't wait!

Suggested also is to organize important documents while you are still in a healthy mind. Express your desires to your children about ceremonial death procedures. Consider a "do not resuscitate" order. Studies show that people who are resuscitated die after one month.

Another reminder is that banks can take over bill paying for those who are handicapped.

You will find helpful documentation of every aspect of life support and sources for help in this book, but I want to conclude with what is true for everyone—the ill and the well who want to live free of pain and in a healthful atmosphere: laughter is free medicine!

Tadd offers many scientific studies that have shown that laughter heals the mind and the body. Perhaps the most famous incident of using laughter for therapeutic purposes is the story of Norman Cousins, who wrote *Anatomy of an Illness*. One could say that he is responsible for putting laughter into the healing repertoire. After leaving a hospital and checking into a hotel, Cousins watched videos of the Marx brothers and *Candid Camera* and took large doses of vitamin C. He found that several hours of intense laughter alleviated his pain for a few hours at a time, and he could finally catch some desperately needed sleep. Armed with just laughter and vitamin C, he recovered from a potentially fatal disease.

Esther C. Gropper

When we laugh, the body releases endorphins, which act as our own internal supply of morphine. And unbeknownst to Cousins, endorphins also boost the immune system. Because hearty laughter affects the body's chemistry positively in ways similar to exercise, Cousins referred to it as "inner jogging."

As Maria Tadd said, "You don't stop laughing because you grow old. You grow old because you stop laughing."

* Added to commentary on Dr. Ian Smith, also read works by John O'Donohue.

> On life's vast ocean diversely we sail;
> Reason the card, but Passion is the gale.
> -Alexander Pope

Passion and Perseverance

Stella Munchick, in her starched whites, witnessed dying and death close at hand. She was affected deeply by one particular scene she witnessed: when the husband of a woman, terminally ill from breast cancer, came to the door of his wife's hospital room, looked in on her, and totally lost his composure.

"Throughout my nursing career, I realized that family members and caregivers had a very tough time dealing with illness and death," she said. "They were virtually ignored." The cumulative impact was disturbingly embedded in Stella's professional experience and was to direct the course of later events in Stella's life.

Stella learned about the hospice movement while taking a course at Florida Atlantic University, where she was pursuing a bachelor's degree in health services. Stella did some research and learned that Cicely Saunders in London, in the sixties, had introduced a service called hospice with favorable response. Here in the United States, two units were already in operation.

This is what we need in every state, Stella thought. This was the inspiration she had been seeking to answer the angst of the last stages of life. But a staff nurse isn't empowered to initiate such a program, nor does she have an organization behind her to promote a program. Nor did she find, as a social worker, that she had the influence needed to start. She needed power behind her to sanction the project. She needed medical credibility. Determined, she went after that despite the fact that she was not asking for money. She envisioned this as home-directed assistance on a volunteer basis.

In the summer of 1977, Stella learned of a conference of funeral directors in Palm Beach County and learned that the director of the Marin County Hospice was to be their featured speaker. She requested a short meeting with him in which she learned that a hospice facility had to have a doctor heading up the unit. She went to the Health Department and talked with the director, Carl Brumback, who responded favorably and introduced her to Dr. James Howell, his associate public health director. He approached the CEO of the Palm Beach Executive Committee with Stella's request to have John F. Kennedy Hospital distribute hospice brochures to families of terminal patients. They were the first to respond.

Her next move was to recruit a medical executive. She went to the director of the American Medical Society, who gave her the names of two retired doctors. The first, Dr. Isio Wasserman of Columbia University, seventy-two years old, liked the idea. He came to Florida, took the exam for the Florida license (although that was not necessary for this plan), passed, and became the mentor ready to advise patients, respond to questions, and act as a very dedicated administrator.

There were other criteria to meet before Stella's plan could come to fruition. Pastoral counseling was required. Bill Brooks of the Mental Health Association helped Stella in many ways, but it was her own husband, Harold Monchick, who invited her to a professional function where she met Father D'Agostino, PhD. He was the psychiatric social worker at St. Michael's College, and he agreed to act as pastoral counselor. Harold Monchick was the treasurer of the Health Association, which incorporated the Palm Beach Hospice as a nonprofit organization.

When Stella was told that they needed to have a nurse on staff, she acted in that capacity and as director of volunteers until they had money to pay somebody. The *Palm Beach Post* ran a full story of the activity that Stella Monchick had undertaken. Her project aroused responses from volunteers, from which she acquired a secretary and a part-time nurse. Others were willing to participate in training for home visits to the very ill terminal patients to give care and solace to the patient and family and to enlist assistance from other staff members as needed. In

1979, they served their first patient, a young mother with breast cancer, at her home.

Word spread of this noble project, and in January of 1979, Dr. Tom Murphy told his friend Noreen McKeen about Stella's work. She responded with a contribution of $5,000, which financed an office, telephones, and units in hospitals.

In the midst of this developing organization, Harold Monchick was diagnosed with an irremediable brain tumor. Upon his death, Stella Monchick set up a Hospice Educational Endowment Fund with the Community Foundation of Palm Beach and Martin County that affords some income to the organization. Ironically, when she had originally requested funding from the Community Fund, she had been turned down because she couldn't provide balancing funds.

In September 1979, Catherine MacArthur contributed $50,000. The president of the Community Fund, Mr. Kelly, came from Chicago to Palm Beach to investigate and interview the principals of hospice and gave his approval. The hospice service was now able to give small salaries for a full-time professional nurse and other needed help. In 1981, they ran out of money, and Mrs. MacArthur endowed them with three million dollars.

In 1998, Stella Monchick West, now remarried, retired from the hospice, knowing that Medicare had started to reimburse the hospice for services. She left knowing her organization was stable; well-trained and compassionate volunteers would continue this noble practice.

Stella had one final tribute to make to Cicely Saunders, whose concept of hospice had taken root in London. For that woman's great contribution to humanity around the world, Ms. Saunders was knighted by the Queen of England.

Esther C. Gropper

> **Even the woodpecker owes his success**
> **To the fact that he uses his head and keeps pecking away**
> **Until he finishes the job.**
> **Coleman Cox**

One Inspired Person Affects a County

How often have you heard someone say, "He's following in his father's footsteps" or "He's stepping into his father's boots"? More to the point that I have been making is, how have people who started life with profound disadvantages become people we admire and would emulate? I have offered research that indicates that we are born predisposed toward optimism or pessimism, yet we are given the will and the power to change those proclivities. How, for instance, do you read "Mama's Shoes" without wondering about the future of the child?

Mama's Shoes

The leaves have turned, the
Days are brisk,
Feelings somber, daylight
Shorter.
I feel a change, subtle, but all
The while.
Emptiness creeps in, reminiscent
Of my "child."
The darkness inside equal only
To the outside
Remind me of the years alone
And waiting
For my Mama to return home,
Her body aching.

Most times, her heart still breaking.
Waiting! Waiting! The cold is
Penetrating.
One bus, another, then another.
So, so, lonely.
This one, for certain, is it her
Or is it only
An illusion of my Mama's feet
I see from across the street?
Mama, Mama, you are my whole world,

I know how much you love me.
You call me "your little girl."
It's 7:30, and it's so late! Did something happen? No, wait!
It's her; it's her? Are those her shoes
from under the bus,
Within my view?

Her face lights up as the bus rolls by.
She sees me waving. I could cry.
That darkness inside disappears and it's
Much warmer now
'cause Mama's here to soothe my fears.

This was written by Florence Morgenstern, the force behind the success of the Community Arts Festival in Palm Beach County, Florida. The story of her life is built on perseverance, a word in my lexicon that is synonymous with *backbone*: each vertebra reinforced with determination to beat the enemy.

Abandoned at birth by her father, Florence was left with her unskilled mother to provide for and nurture a six-year-old and an infant to maturity. The odds would be against distinction, but the older

Gilda became a teacher; Florence, or *Fageleh* (tender bird), as her mother called her, became a businesswoman extraordinaire, multifaceted artist, community organizer, and producer of the highly successful Community Performing Arts Series in Palm Beach County.

It just didn't happen, nor did it happen without pain and determination. Gilda was old enough to go to school, but what do you do with an infant when you have to provide for children? Florence, as an infant, was bundled up in her carriage and placed outside the fish store where her mother worked ten to twelve hours a day. The weather at one time was so threatening that when an insurance man came into the store, Florence's mother begged him to take the children home in his car. When she returned home, she saw the apartment window in darkness. What had happened to her children? Had the insurance man kidnapped them? Her heart beating like a conga drum, she ran upstairs to the two attic rooms they occupied, to find the two kids huddled in a corner, trying to keep each other warm. The electricity was turned off. Mama couldn't pay the bill.

Sometimes, the mother could provide day care; sometimes, they had to move temporarily in with relatives. Florrie remembers sleeping on an improvised bed of chairs. For a while, Gilda was sent to relatives who made certain she went to school. When Florrie started school, she found it a haven. Bright and pretty, Florrie was liked by her teachers, often favored for the special tasks that kids love to be asked to do by teachers.

Did the other kids like that? Did they want her as a friend? No, she was shunned. "You're always smiling!" ridiculed one or another.

Her mother, wise and wily to the threats of the streets, arranged piano lessons at half price for one, with the second one free. How she managed dance lessons or Hebrew classes still bewilders. But Florrie put them all to use in the years ahead. First off, she kept warm waiting for her mother at the bus stop every evening by tapping out the routines she had learned in class. In school, she began to play the piano with the school orchestra. She received art instruction and anything else

Dance until the Music Stops

her mother could devise to keep the child out of trouble. Despite full afternoons, she was a lonely child, always cold and alone in dark rooms! Her poem tells it more poignantly than I do.

Deprivation trailed behind her, a forbidding shadow whispering of uncertainty ahead. Nonetheless, when at seventeen, she married Seymour, her future brightened. She considered herself his partner in making their marriage work. After her daughter was born ten months later, she had two sons, but she looked forward to the time when, like her mother, she could take some of the family's financial burden onto herself. Before long, she was applying to Manpower for temporary jobs, but remembering her mother's absences, she started a nursery school at home. She was there with milk and cupcakes when her children came home from school.

Later, with her sister and brother-in-law, Florrie opened a summer camp. Seymour was always cooperative. When her sister, after seven years, took off for Israel, leaving Florrie and Seymour to fend for themselves, she said, "Well, it doesn't matter how many times you fall off the horse; it's how many times you get back up on the horse." They ran the camp themselves.

Living in Pittsfield, a music and recreation center that beckoned tourists and settlers, Florrie, with her astute marketing attributes, opened the first of three Mad Mad World boutique shops. Her keen sense of design and style found fast favor, leading to two bridal shops, and later two more shops. Her greatest problem, she admitted, was shoplifters. She soon overcame this by setting up an electronic system.

This happy phase of her life was disrupted when Florrie developed lymphoma. After enduring treatment, she emerged determined to work again, to go on with her life. She sold the shops and moved to an adult community in New Jersey. "We had great tennis games, new companions, and great conversations, but I felt this intense inner drive to work in the creative arts."

Her home is a museum of her talents. Her vibrantly painted canvases and sculptures on framework she constructed are unique contemporary expressions. Against one wall is a grandfather clock that she assembled herself, inner works and all, enclosing it in a case that features her stained-glass designs. She designed porcelain dolls with her own original heads and costumes; she organized Two Cents Plain, a Klezmer musical group; she taught herself the accordion and performed for many community groups. Beading fascinated her. Her unusual strings and artful combinations of gems sold as quickly as she completed them. There is hardly an art form that she hasn't explored and mastered.

Florrie's mind, eyes, and hands never stop generating beautiful objects, but in my mind, her greatest achievement, measured in the pleasure she affords to thousands of people, is community performing arts: thirty-five concerts this year, with a projected forty for 2012 at the Spanish River Church Auditorium in Delray, Florida. After attending concerts at major centers, she wondered why good concerts couldn't be offered at affordable prices for the music and art lovers around the county. How could this be done without venture capital to spur her on her way?

She recruited people in her community. Seven hundred favorably responded by giving her checks for a first series of four concerts. This gave her the impetus to approach neighboring communities, where, again, a warm reception was forthcoming.

She fulfilled her promise but not before she managed to secure a viable concert hall—one convenient to the communities, with enough seating and with good acoustics. When she was told that only varied Monday nights were available, she seized the dates—with a bit of apprehension, of course.

Did she have experience in programming, ticket distribution, lighting, staging, or the multitude of details that go into performances? No! But this is no ordinary woman. She learns quickly and inspires profoundly. Many volunteered their time and services. And never to be discounted was her enthusiasm and her basic principle: whenever she met with possible contributors and volunteers, she made it clear that she would brook no negativity. Anyone with that attitude was excused, but

Dance until the Music Stops

before anyone could say *thanks*, 1,500 people signed up. On Monday, January 2002, the auditorium filled up, and the evening was a complete success. How else could it be? The series offered the Florida Philharmonic Orchestra; the Symphony of the Americas, Ballet Florida, the Dallas Blues, a well-designed, acoustically suited auditorium with comfortable seats, good parking, good location, and best of all, affordable cost.

Even though they lost their deposit on contract with the Florida Philharmonic, which disbanded before the second year's series, Florrie managed another successful year. Demand for tickets grew, and a second series was planned.

During the third year, Florrie took seriously ill. Her devoted son, Jeffrey, an electrical engineer, metaphorically mounted his white horse, galloped down the turnpike, and took over. He installed a rotating seating system to stem criticism about favored seating, installed two large side screens for enhanced visual effects, had a dance stage fitted, and set up identifiable color-coded sections. Traffic flowed easily. Mother and son are constantly evaluating and assessing performances.

Florence slowly recovered and again walks on stage, beautifully attired, regal in appearance, smiling and warmly greeting subscribers at each performance. She continues to manage what has been, up to this point, with seven series during the season, a nonprofit venture. The future is bright. Next year, their eighth, they will have eight series and three optional presentations. By 2013, they project ten series. Greater demands pour in for tickets to these favorably priced series comprised of highly performing artists. Perhaps the endeavor will become a for-profit company. All of which, Florence admits, she could not do without the love and support from her husband, Seymour, and her family.

This woman is one truly remarkable senior citizen who never flickers or flounders, who persevered against life's greatest obstacles and was determined to give her talents to community pioneer projects. People like her have spunk! They give adversity a helpful and promising role to play. They give heroic gifts that contribute to culture and stability. They make American civilization what it is: a standard to the world. It

Esther C. Gropper

is a very high standard for pioneering generations of seniors to follow in the future. They illustrate the potential for enriched living in our older years.

Because I'd like to leave you with a smile, I share a moment with Bluma and Bob:

Bluma was watching the shuffling of candidates as the election year approached. "What would you do, Bob, if you were elected president?"

"Demand a recount! That denied, I would quote Shakespeare: The times are out of joint."

Dance until the Music Stops

1. CALLED THE INTELLECTUALS
From left to right: BLUMA SCHWARZ-ROBERT SCHWARZ-ESTHER GROPPER- SIDNEY MELLMAN-PAULA CHALEF-MORT CHALEF-SYLVIA KREITZBERG, ABE BRESLOV, EVELYN & BRUCE RABISON

2. TRACEY DOWNING
Torchbearer in the Olympics 2002   SEE: Memoirs

Dance until the Music Stops

3. LEARNING TO DANCE WITH THE MUSIC
second from right: JORDAN MUSHTALER, My great granddaughter

Esther C. Gropper

4. Professor ROBERT SCHWARZ ever ready with a quip or a lecture.

5. BLUMA SCHWARZ, a gracious understanding facilitator.

Esther C. Gropper

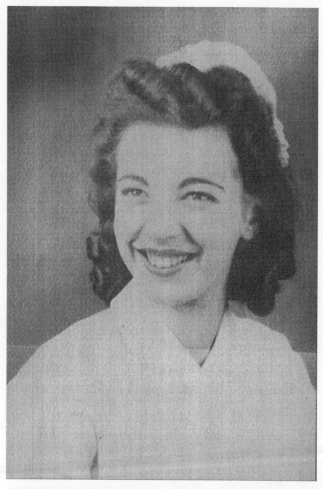

6. STELLA MUNCHICK WEST as a white-capped nurse

Dance until the Music Stops

7. PINKY FAIRCHILD beside one of her monthly topical stage paintings in the auditorium of her residence.

Esther C. Gropper

8. FLORENCE and SIDNEY MORGENSTERN at their 40th Anniversary Party

Dance until the Music Stops

9. JULIA L. BLOCHER with her dancing teacher when she was 86. She danced at his studio every week, performed with her dance group into her 90's.

Esther C. Gropper

10. ESTHER WITH HER THREE CHILDREN: ROBERT (left of her) MALCOLM and LAUREL to the right)

Dance until the Music Stops

11. GREAT GRANDMA ESTHER TAKING DANCING LESSONS FROM JORDAN and LAUREN MUSHTALER

Esther C. Gropper

12. ESTHER with PROFESSOR BARNEY FELDMAN, her second husband. 1960

13. ESTHER with DR, FRANK MAGID, her companion and advisor on the book.

Esther C. Gropper

14. BERT GROPPER (A) Happiness is a five trout catch

(B) BERT on a country walk.

15. SHIRLEY AND MORT WEISS 1982

About the Author

During the WWII years, I arranged for a nanny while I went back to my position as a promotional executive with a large lingerie firm. I worked on radio commercials and had early experience with television. I did the correct thing by retiring from that to raise a family of three. During those years, I felt drawn to media, returned to college, finished the remaining three years toward my degree cum laude by attending evening classes. The death of my husband necessitated income. I became a teacher and guidance counselor. I earned a master's degree and professional degree in linguistics, and I published articles in journals of the experimental curriculum I initiated in high-school and college courses. My articles have appeared in *Literary Criticism, English Journal,* and *New York State English Journal.* I received an award for creative writing from New York State and had my articles excerpted for research at the Library of Congress. Once retired, I pursued a freelance writer's career, successfully publishing several articles and receiving awards for stories and poems. I have taught creative writing for the Center for Lifetime Learning at Palm Beach Community College, published anthologies of the students' works, and become president of the organization, initiating many programs there. I shared the strains and stresses of juggling career, marriage, and an active household with three children. Those children, my four grandchildren, and my seven great-grandchildren fill my life with pleasure.

Acknowledgments

My associations and relationships, particularly in an environment of retirees these past thirty years, have made me aware of mature personalities and characteristics of people in their own new age of extended life. This has been a rich and enriched life for me. I have met extremely interesting and talented people; I have learned more from them than from the cloistered academic life I had led the previous twenty years. I have found my interests broadened and receptivity challenged. I am grateful to any I have mentioned in this book, but I am extremely blessed in the friendships of Professor Robert and Bluma Schwarz and that of my dear companion, Frank Magid, PhD, who inspired and collaborated with me through this process.

Robert (Bob) Schwarz was born in Vienna, Austria. His life had been a struggle through adversity, mired in obstacles, through which he emerged as a noble advocate of humanity and model of civilized man. He was saved by the Kindertransport train from the hell of Nazi iniquity, sheltered in England, and later mercifully reunited with his family in Atlanta, Georgia, where he was able to continue his education. He received highest honors for scholastic academic achievement, Phi Beta Kappa. As a professor, he received the Faculty Award for Excellence in Undergraduate Instruction from Florida Atlantic University, as well as recognition from outstanding fraternities and academic centers around the world. Besides teaching philosophy and history, he has written prolifically. He has worldwide commendations for his papers on history and philosophy; he has authored over three hundred book reviews related to infamous Nazis as well as the great philosophers, on the geopolitical impact of Austrian and German history. He has been invited to teach in higher institutions of learning in Austria, Kenya, the United Kingdom, Germany, Mexico and Italy. He continues to lecture from his encyclopedic memory of history, philosophy and world literature with clarity and wit.

Bluma Bretstein Schwarz, a native of Rochester, New York, earned her BA in sociology in 1944 and received her MA in clinical psychology in 1946 at Syracuse University. She met Robert while he was there studying for his PhD. They were married on April 3, 1946. She became an instructor of English composition at University of Wisconsin and an instructor of freshman English at Carnegie Mellon University during Bob's tenure at that institute. When they moved to Florida, she joined the Center for Group Counseling as a group therapist and counselor coordinator. She served as outpatient director from 1974 to 1977 and then went into private practice as a psychotherapist. She has done guest lecturing at senior centers. She and Bob have a daughter, Claire, who embodies the fine values of her parents.

Dr. Frank Magid was born on September 12, 1921, one year after his paternal clan came to Ellis Island. They endured hunger and very narrow escapes from death at the hands of marauding bands of Ukrainians, White Russians, Cossacks, and then Red Russians. His weltanschuauung, or worldview, was shaped by stories oft repeated about those events at weekly gatherings of the clan.

When Frank was fifteen, his father was diagnosed with tuberculosis and sent to a sanitarium. He never recovered. The oldest of four boys, Frank became the man of the family.

As a young boy, Frank excelled in street sports, such as two-hand touch football. He also did well at all school subjects except art and music. He loved writing. Desperate to go to college, he tried for and won the Mayor's Scholarship in Philadelphia, Pennsylvania, and also the City Scholarship—each for four years at any university in the United States, admission guaranteed. He also won a State Senator Scholarship, which paid for books and miscellaneous items. He chose the University of Pennsylvania because of a job offer in the library and because of the school's proximity to home. He achieved Phi Beta Kappa awards and joined German and political honorary Societies.

One week after graduation, he was in the Army infantry. At the end of his service, he was with his division, invading southern France. He was one of the first to reach and liberate the Dachau concentration camp.

Back home, he enrolled again at the University of Penn under the GI Bill, graduating with his PhD in clinical psychology. While attending, he worked from 4:00 p.m. to midnight for necessary funds. He was employed by the Jewish Family Services in Philadelphia, where he started the Family Life Education Program. He then went to the Boston Jewish Family and Children's Services. Subsequently, he became Director of the Tri-City Community Mental Health Clinic, where he practiced until 1985. He then established his own private practice. He became consultant lecturer and adjunct Professor at two nursing schools and graduate schools of psychiatry, where med students did three months of psychiatric rotation.

He was married for forty-five years to Claire, who died of lymphoma in 1995. He has two daughters, Deborah and Barbara, both career women. He moved to Lakeside Village, a senior residence, in July 2008, where "I fell in love with Esther. Her name means 'star'—and she outshines them all!"

Esther C. Gropper

A special thanks to Bob, Bluma, and Frank for their encouragement and contributions to my book and my life. They have given substance to my thesis that an extended life span can be rich and remarkable.

I owe a note of thanks to Jane Sample, who became more than an assistant with my manuscript. She worked me through the mysteries of advanced computing that today's writing entails. She is an avid gardener and nature guide for our beautiful parks and reservations. Her love for plants, birds, and animals shines through.

I have to express deep thanks to my son Malcolm for the many impositions on his time and patience as he guided me through the intricacies of electronic comnputor processses that publishing now requires. I could not have completed this project without him.

References

Amen, Daniel G. M. *Change Your Brain, Change Your Life*. New York: Three Rivers Press, 1998.

Boggs, Grace. *Living For Change: A Biography*. University of Minnesota Press, 1998.

Cohen, Gene D. *The Mature Mind*. Thorndike Press, 2007.

Davis, Wade. *Book of Peoples of the World: A Guide to Cultures*. National Geographic Society, 2008.

Goleman, Daniel. *Emotional Intelligence*. Bantam Press.

Imber, Gerald. *Genius on the Edge*. New York: Kaplan Publishing.

Maurer, Robert. *One Small Step Can Change Your Life: The Kaizen Way*. New York: Workman Publishing.

O'Donohue, John. *Anam Cara: A Book of Celtic Wisdom*. New York: HarperCollins.

Smith, Ian, *Happy*. St. Martin's Griffin, Dec. 2010.

Tadd, Maria. *Happiness Is Growing Old at Home*. Chapel Hill, NC: Terrapin Press.

The Best Years of Your Life: Everything You Need to Know Now to Plan for the Years Ahead. Stanford, CT: Bottom Line Books, 2002.

Index

Symbols

100th Birthday celebrant 141

A

AARP findings on lifestyles 104
Alterman, Frieda MD. 61

B

Bernier, Rosamond 47
Braunfeld, Judy Gerentologist 161
Braunfeld, Peter 173
Brel, Jacques 1

C

Changing mores 65
Cohen, G. D. MD.
   The Mature Mind 48
Community Arts Festival Founder: Florence Morgenstern 193
Cousins, Norman
   Anatomy of an Illness 187

D

Dating systems 125
Davis, Wade
   Book of Peoples of the World: A Guide to Cultures 173
Downing, Tracey
   The Journey: The Experience of Becoming an Ironwoman 94

E

Elder abuse 146
Expectations 17, 24, 81

F

Five domains emotional intelligence in 169
Frau Charlotte Schiller 54
Freud, Sigmund 130

Esther C. Gropper

G

Gellman, Rabbi 56
Generational life 1
Goleman, David MD.
  Emotional Intelligence 62
Gropper, Esther C.
  Not Far From The Tree 60

H

Halper, Evelyn (dancer, lecturer) 177
Halsted, William Stewart MD. 130
Happiest moments 49
Hawaiian Proclamation: Lucille Rosenthal Day 150
Hints to Start Your Day 142
Hospice 54, 189, 189–192, 190, 191

I

Imber, Gerald MD.
  Genuis on the Edge 130
Infidelity 55, 56

K

Kantor, Jodi
  The First Marriage 69

L

Leto, Philip JD 77
Loh, Sandra Tsing
  My So Called Wife 67
Longevity study (Benedict Cary, Dr. Claudia Kawass) 19

M

MacArthur, Catherine 191
Magid, Frank PhD 217
Mama's Shoes 192
Marlowe, Edythe 93
Masters and Johnson (studies) 129
Maurer, Robert PhD
  One Small Step Can Change Your Life: The Kaizen Way 20
May, Rollo 157
McKeen, Noreen 191
Memoirs/Memory 27, 36, 93

Munchick, Stella 189
Murphy, Tom MD. 191

O

Obama, Barack and Michelle 69
O'Donohue, John
  Anam Cara 116, 154, 188
One Small Step Can Change Your Life 20, 221

P

Patience and determination 25
Pinsky, Robert (Poet Laureate) 165

R

Rabbi Gellman 56
Ress, Etta 93

S

Saunders, Cicely (Hon. Knighted) 191
Schwarz, Bluma 199, 203, 217
Schwarz, Fred 42
Schwarz, Robert PhD. 42
Smith, Ian K.
  Happy 183, 188
Social skills 32
Sunshine and Rain in the Ebbing Years 89

T

Tadd, Maria
  Happiness Is Growing Old at Home 186, 188

W

Weiss, Mort 148